Reykjavik

Richard Bean

methuen | drama

LONDON · NEW YORK · OXFORD · NEW DELHI · SYDNEY

METHUEN DRAMA
Bloomsbury Publishing Plc
50 Bedford Square, London, WC1B 3DP, UK
1385 Broadway, New York, NY 10018, USA
29 Earlsfort Terrace, Dublin 2, Ireland

BLOOMSBURY, METHUEN DRAMA and the Methuen
Drama logo are trademarks of Bloomsbury Publishing Plc

First published in Great Britain 2024

Cover design: Shaun Webb, SWD Design

A catalogue record for this book is available from the British Library.

A catalog record for this book is available from the Library of Congress.

ISBN: PB: 978-1-350-54469-7
ePDF: 978-1-350-54471-0
eBook: 978-1-350-54470-3

Series: Modern Plays

Typeset by Mark Heslington Ltd, Scarborough, North Yorkshire

To find out more about our authors and books visit
www.bloomsbury.com and sign up for our newsletters.

Reykjavik, a new play by Richard Bean, premiered at London's Hampstead Theatre on 18 October 2024 with the following cast and creative team:

Charlotte/Einhildur	**Sophie Cox**
Reverend Wallace Polkinghorne/Jack	**Matthew Durkan**
Lizzie Jopling	**Laura Elsworthy**
William Claxton/Quayle	**Paul Hickey**
Donald Claxton	**John Hollingworth**
Ricky Toov/Snacker	**Adam Hugill**
Baggie	**Matt Sutton**

Director	Emily Burns
Designer	Anna Reid
Lighting Designer	Oliver Fenwick
Sound Designer	Christopher Shutt
Composer	Grant Olding
Dialect	Mary Howland
Fight Director	MC_Combat (Maisie Carter)
Casting Director	Bryony Jarvis-Taylor

Acknowledgements

I was helped in my research by Ruth Creasey of STAND – St Andrew's Dock Heritage Park Action Group. I'd like to thank Keith Gay for allowing us to develop and use for our own purposes his song 'Arthur So Long'. Keith's uncle, Phil Gay, is a legend for his last words. Victor Wheeldon informed me of how ship-to-shore communication worked via Wick Radio. Norman Drydale told me a different fishy tale every night during my year working in the Wonderloaf bakery in Wheeler Street, Hull. I never met Walter Denton – aka Dillinger – but I'd like to thank him for his mad life which birthed a thousand stories, some of which I've retold. Francis Magee shared with me his 'Ramsey Thing' experience. I'd like to thank the Hull Bullnose Heritage Group and the Hull Fishing Heritage Centre for their fabulous museum and the generosity and time given to the creatives on this production. I'd like to thank Jonathan Watson Hall for his time and honesty.

The development of this play has been supported by Matthew Warchus and the Old Vic Theatre, the Royal National Theatre and Hampstead Theatre. Gyda Jonsdottir was a massive help in all things Icelandic.

Those who were lost will not be forgotten.

Reykjavik

Characters (in order of appearance)

In Hull:

Donald Claxton, *fifty*
Charlotte, *sixteen*
William Claxton, *seventy-five*
Ricky Toov, *twenty-five*
Lizzie Jopling, *thirty-three*
Reverend Wallace Polkinghorne, *twenty-five*

In Reykjavik:

Jack, *thirty*
Baggie, *forty*
Snacker, *nineteen*
Einhildur, *twenty-one*
Donald Claxton, *fifty*
Quayle, *fifty*

Set

For Hull – the offices of Claxton Line, a distant-water trawling operation. A speaker is mounted on the wall which amplifies calls from the ships via Wick Radio station. Stage right is Claxton's desk which faces the stage-right wall so that when Claxton is seated his back is to the room. Stage left, another desk, more modest, with typewriter. Filing cabinets and files. The back wall is a large glass window looking out on to the dock, but since it's black outside and inside is lit, we can't see out.

For Reykjavik – the lobby and bar area of the Hotel Spuggi in Reykjavik, Iceland, February 1976. An open area upstage suggests an entrance to a restaurant room.

Lighting

For Hull it's February and night. For Reykjavik it's also February and permanent night.

Hull

February 1976, early evening, and already dark outside. The lights of the dock are discernible through the upstage glass window, but because of the lights in the office we can't see through the window. The offices of Claxton Line distant-water trawling company in Hull. **Donald Claxton** *is sat at his desk looking at paperwork. A ship's horn sounds, long and mournful. He stands and goes to the glass, and placing his head against the glass and his eyes shielding the light, he peers through the glass. Then he sits. A buzzer goes on his desk. He touches the phone to allow communication with* **Charlotte**.

Claxton   Yes, Charlotte?

Charlotte (*off/distort*)   A link call through Wick.

Claxton   What ship?

Charlotte   The *George Eliot*.

Claxton   Yes, put them through.

He presses another button on the phone which relays the phone call through a speaker on the wall. He then stands and chalks up items of information on a chalk-board diary of market days.

Wick Radio (*voiceover/Scottish accent*)   Wick Radio here. I have the FV *George Eliot* call sign Golf Foxtrot Zulu on the FT. I can patch him in and make a link call? All link calls charged to the ship in gold francs.

Claxton   Yes, thank you, we'll take it, thank you.

It is patched in so an increase in distort.

Sammy (*voiceover*)   Are you receiving?

Claxton   Loud and clear.

Sammy   Is that you, Percy?

Claxton   No, skipper. This is Donald Claxton.

Sammy   Oh. Hello, Mister Claxton. Where's Percy?

Claxton   He's taken the day off. Where are you?

Sammy   I'm off Stonehaven. What do you want me to do? The control ship sent a code in last night's sched' but I got no reply.

Claxton   Percy.

Sammy   Aye, I guess.

Claxton   What do you have?

Sammy   About twelve hundred kit of cod, and seven hundred dux.

Claxton   Nice lot of haddock, eh?

Sammy   Beautiful big fish an'all.

Claxton   Where have you been?

Sammy   Iceland. Hari Kari, Cigar Bank and Working Bank.

Claxton   You didn't fancy the west coast then?

Sammy   I seen that weather coming.

Claxton   When can you get here?

Sammy   The plan was Wednesday.

Claxton   We've got the *Charles Dickens* coming in for Wednesday. Also, a lot of haddock. Sit out for a night and come in for Thursday.

Sammy   Argh. The lads won't like that. It's been fucking rough. I've worked 'em like dogs.

Claxton   If you come in for Wednesday that'll kill the market. Sit out one night, the price will still be good. More money for you and the crew.

Sammy   I could go to Grimsby, for Wednesday.

Claxton   Skipper, I don't want you going to Grimsby.

Sammy   Aye, aye. The third hand brok' his foot.

Claxton   How?

Sammy   Big stone.

Claxton   Was he fucking about?

Sammy   Letting out the cod end.

Claxton   Lucky it was only his foot then.

Sammy   That's what I told him.

Claxton   See you Thursday, skip.

Sammy   Aye, aye, Mr Claxton. Wick Radio over and out.

Wick Radio   Wick Radio, that link call was one minute thirty-seven. The charge to the *George Eliot* call sign Golf Foxtrot –

Claxton *flicks a button and the call ends. He walks towards the door and turns the office lights off. We can now see the dock, with rows and rows of sidewinders moored up. He looks out, surveys his kingdom. Enter* **Charlotte**. *She screams a gentle scream, a response to the dark office. She is a young woman in the fashions of the day.*

Charlotte (*little scream*)   Sorry. It's dark.

Claxton   It's the only way I can see out.

He turns a desk light on.

You should go home, Charlotte.

Charlotte   Here's the list. For the vicar.

Claxton   Good. Can you do maybe ten copies?

Charlotte   Ten?

Claxton   When's the vicar coming?

Charlotte   He said six o'clock.

Claxton   I've not met this one. I hear he's a communist.

Charlotte   He's lovely. He married my sister. You know, I mean, he didn't marry her, he married her, if you know what I mean. He's really young, bit of a hippy. Funny. Doesn't seem old enough to marry anyone or bury anyone.

It's as if she can't hand over the list.

Claxton   Can I see the list?

Charlotte   The Snacker asked me out. But I don't know his name.

Claxton   Neither do I. But I do know he's not on here. He survived.

Charlotte   Oh God! Thank God for that! Oh lo'r's!

Claxton   Did you go out with him?

Charlotte   No. My mam wouldn't have it.

Claxton   She wasn't happy with you getting this job was she?

Charlotte   No. Thinks it's a bit of a rough do. Fishing. She's dead worried I might marry one of them. Ha! There's no fishing in our family you see.

Claxton   You're still at home then?

Charlotte   Yes, Gipsyville.

Claxton   You'll need to come with us to Holy Trinity, it's important that the staff are seen to be there.

Charlotte   Oh lo'r's! I haven't got anything proper to wear.

Claxton   I'll sub you the money.

Charlotte   When is it?

Claxton   That's for the vicar to decide. Won't be for a week. Get yourself to Hammonds, find something you like. Sober.

Charlotte   Thank you. If I'm staying over my hours to do the list, tonight –

Claxton – that's overtime. Thank you. I won't be in the office tomorrow, I'm doing the walk.

Charlotte Tomorrow?

Claxton Yes. I'll be back in Thursday presuming I survive the walk intact.

Charlotte Oh lo'r's! That sounds horrible.

Claxton It's a great and noble tradition.

Charlotte How am I doing? Just that, I've got a few things wrong and –

Claxton – you're learning. It's an unusual business. But you're doing well. Your typing is good. Your telephone manner is excellent. Are you enjoying it?

Charlotte I'm a bit scared of everything, everyone. I keep thinking I'm going to fall in the dock.

Claxton Can you swim?

Charlotte No.

Claxton So if you do fall in, hold your breath, and when you hit the bottom, walk to the side, and climb out.

Charlotte Right.

Claxton Fishing. It's primal. Mythic. It's hunting.

Charlotte Yes, I never thought of it like that.

William Claxton *enters. He is a man of about seventy-five. He is wearing an old three-piece suit and good leather shoes. He walks with a stick. He sits at a little desk, his desk, which is less of a functioning desk and more of a nod to what he once was. Neither* **Donald** *nor* **Charlotte** *speak to him.*

Charlotte That young skipper is still outside. Do you want me to keep him waiting? He's been out there for over an hour.

Claxton Let's give him a bit longer shall we.

Charlotte   Why are you keeping him waiting? As you say, I'm learning. Is it because you're gonna sack him?

Claxton   It's not because I'm going to sack him, that I've kept him waiting, although I will sack him, it's because I want him to have time to think about why I'm sacking him.

Charlotte   Oh, I see. That's very clever.

She leaves.

Claxton   Where have you been?

William   Down to the Bull Nose and back. Seen a few folks.

Claxton   Shown your face.

William   Aye. I'd say it's been appreciated.

Claxton   How did you cope, Dad? Times like this.

William   You've got to learn to close your heart.

Silence.

Claxton   Thanks. Useful advice.

William   The community, they know it's no one's fault. It's fate. The sea. Weather. You get hardened to it.

Claxton   Why did you come in today?

William   It's important to not hide away. Put yourself about the dock.

Claxton   You're addicted. To the tragedy and comedy of fishing.

William   It's all I know. I like being on dock.

Claxton   You're not on dock, you're in my office. You think about fishing twenty-four hours a day. You're retired. You should be playing golf.

William   I were a never a toff.

Claxton   Crown green bowls.

William   Can't get down that low.

Claxton   Snooker.

William   I'm colour blind.

During the next **Claxton** *busies himself with paperwork and occasionally chucks in a pensioner's hobby, but there are big gaps in between.*

Claxton   Bee keeping. Growing tomatoes. Bridge – might meet a woman. Origami. Glass blowing. Marathon running.

William *finds an estate agent's brochure.*

William   What's this?

Claxton   Not now, Dad.

William   Four hundred and ninety-nine thousand pounds. That's five hundred thousand really.

Claxton   I'm thinking of moving.

William (*reading*)   Cranswick Hall.

Claxton   Yes.

William   Where is it?

Claxton   Cranswick. (*Beat.*) Nine hundred acres.

William   Another farm?

Claxton   Not a farm no, an estate.

William   Cranswick's twenty mile out of town. And I don't drive.

Claxton   I know.

William   You'll have to give me a lift in every day.

Claxton   There'll be so much to do out there you won't want to come in.

William (*reading*)   Equestrian facilities?

Claxton   Yes. I quite fancy giving that a go.

William   You don't ride.

Claxton   I'll go on a course. Learn how to do a hill start.

William   It's too big.

Claxton   That's the point. Eight bedrooms, six receptions, five bathrooms, one heated towel rail. It also has a fully stocked lake.

William   I don't like fishing.

Claxton *laughs.*

William   I don't like the country.

Claxton   We already live in the country.

William   I know, I don't like it, it gets dark.

Claxton   If I buy the place, I'll build you a replica dock, a lock pit, with a pub called Rayners.

William   You should have a house up a hill overlooking the dock.

Claxton   There are no hills in Hull. To pass your driving test you have to do a hill start on Park Street Bridge.

William   You're trying to fit in with all them landed fox-hunting trawler owners. We're not like them. We're fishermen.

Claxton   I'm not.

William   I was. Your grandfather was.

Claxton   You wouldn't let me go to sea! 'Over my dead body!'

William   And you should thank me for that.

Claxton   You can't have it both ways! You're like a miner who wouldn't let his son go down pit, and then constantly reminds him that he's soft.

William   When are you doing the walk?

Claxton   Tomorrow. Any advice? Do's and don'ts.

William   Owt they offer you, tek it. A chair. Tek it. Sit. Tea. Tek it. Yes please. Biscuit. Tek it. One biscuit, yes, but never two. Cake. They won't offer you cake. Sit with them. Don't stand over them. You'll be bigger, and taller than all of them. Always sit.

Claxton *unfreezes, turns his chair to face his dad and listens.*

William   Look 'em in the eye, as if you've done nowt wrong, which you haven't. Ignore any children. You can't win with kids. Don't get involved in a conversation with a child. Don't touch any of the women. Not even a handshake. No one's gonna offer to shake your hand any road. You'll have to drink a lot of tea, so you'll need a piss at some point, but don't ever ask to use their toilet. Plan your pisses, because there'll be folk on the road, watching. Think about where the pubs are. There's plenty on Hessle Road, and they'll understand your situation, even expect you to go in, you won't have to buy a pint. But don't go in Criterion, they might give you grief. Rayners is good, Halfway, Inkerman, the Alex Hotel. There's plenty. Just don't ever take a piss in the house of a woman you've made a widow.

Silence.

Claxton   Thanks, Dad.

He turns back to his paperwork. **William** *takes in the chalk-board information.*

William   Where's the *George Eliot*?

Claxton   Off Stonehaven.

William   What market is she going for?

Claxton   I've told her to hang out for a night and come in on Thursday.

William   Where's she been?

Claxton   Iceland. East coast.

William   Is she full?

Claxton   Yup.

William   Cod and dux?

Claxton   Yup.

William   A lot of dux?

Claxton   Yes. And big.

William   She could go to Grimsby.

Claxton   I don't want her going to Grimsby. He's a young skipper with a fresh crew.

William   If –

Claxton   – Dad! You told me once if you've got a good skipper you'll have a full fish room, and if you've got a good mate the fish in that fish room will be in good condition. I want to keep these two men working together, give them some glory. And the only place for glory is your home port. And I'm willing to lose a thousand pounds to achieve that.

William   I don't understand –

Claxton   – Dad, why this constant criticism?

William   I have never criticised you, son, not never –

Claxton   – you have done nothing but criticise every decision I've made since I took over.

William   Name one thing I've criticised.

Claxton   Ha! OK. Converting the *Henry Fielding* to heavy oil.

William   I didn't criticise that.

Claxton   You said it was an old ship, and it was throwing good money after bad.

William   That's not criticism, that's a fact. Have you made your money back?

Claxton   I budget by fleet not by ship.

William   Which is a bloody daft way of budgeting.

Claxton (*flicks the telephone panel*)   Charlotte, could you call a taxi please for my father, he's going home now, and, er . . . send . . . the skipper in, thank you.

William   Are you sacking him? This lad.

Claxton   Yes.

William   Do I know him?

Claxton   No.

William   I'll know his family.

Claxton   I'm sure you will.

William   What's his name?

Claxton   I'm not telling you.

William   I had a skipper once . . . ha, ha, ha. Sacked himself.

Claxton   Get away.

William   Aye. Come home, nowt to show for two weeks in White Sea, he opened that very door there, chucked his log and his papers in, said nowt, and closed the door. Never even come in the office. Ha, ha, ha. Set off on a six-month walkabout! Ha, ha, ha. Sacked himself!

Charlotte *enters with* **Ricky Toov**. **Ricky** *is about twenty-five, handsome to the point of flash.*

Charlotte   Mister Toov for you, sir.

William   So you're Ricky Toov?

Ricky   Yes, sir, Mister Claxton. My father shipped with you. Bosun.

William   Cecil?

Ricky   That's him.

William   How is he?

Ricky   Badly, sir.

William   What is it?

Ricky   Arthritis. Says he's bust every bone in his body.

William   He was always a bugger for exaggerating.

Ricky   Ha, that's him for sure!

Claxton *coughs.*

William   Give him my regards.

Ricky   I will, sir.

William *picks his overcoat off the hook and leaves.* **Charlotte** *closes the door behind her.* **Claxton** *keeps his back to* **Ricky** *and doesn't speak for what feels like an age.* **Ricky** *toughs it out, quite still himself, he knows what he's doing. Silence.*

Claxton   How many kit of cod?

Ricky   Five hundred and thirty-two.

Claxton *writes that down. Silence.*

Claxton   Dux?

Ricky   Nearly two hundred.

Claxton   How many?

Ricky   Hundred and eighty-seven.

Claxton *writes that down. Silence.*

Claxton   Coley?

Ricky   Seventy.

Claxton *writes that down. Silence.*

Claxton   Dogs?

Ricky   Dogs?

Claxton   Woof, woof!

Ricky   What is this? You don't want to know how many dogfish I got?

Claxton   You got fuck-all else.

Ricky   Twennie, twennie-five.

Claxton *writes that down. Then turns to face* **Ricky**.

Claxton   So . . . what have we learned?

Ricky   Dunno. Not good enough I guess.

Claxton   What we've learned is that you couldn't find fish in a fucking fish shop.

Silence.

You nearly had a good trip last trip.

Ricky   The last trip?

Claxton   Do you remember how you fucked it up?

Ricky   No.

Claxton   Every time you found the fish, like a 'pleased with himself twat' you went on the fucking radio and broadcast it to the world. Result?

Ricky   Yeah, yeah, everyone knows where the fish are and –

Claxton   – they fucking catch them! Who do you think you are? Tony fucking Blackburn?

Ricky   I learned mesen that lesson.

Claxton   You work for me so, if you find the fish, they're my fucking fish and I don't want any other fucker thinking they're theirs.

Ricky   I used to be dead chuffed when I found the fish.

Claxton   Ah, so if you're so fucking mentally weak that you need recognition for doing your job –

Ricky   – what?!

Claxton   I said if you're so fucking mentally weak that you need recognition for doing your job, send a telegram to me or Percy telling us how fucking brilliant you are. No one can listen in to a telegram. Do not broadcast on the VHF so every Scrob boat and every Ross bastard from Grimsby can fill their boots with my cod, and my haddock –

Ricky   – your cod, and your haddock?

Claxton   Yes. They fucking are mine if you were using *my* ten thousand pound Marconi Marine Fishgraph 2 fucking fish finder! Do you not understand capitalism?

Ricky   We got a big halibut.

Silence.

Claxton   You've got a six hundred ton trawler, a crew of nineteen, three weeks, a Fishgraph 2 and you've got the nerve to stand there and tell me about *one*, about *one*, *one* fucking fish.

Ricky   It's six foot six and nearly three hundred pound.

Claxton   Has it got a skipper's ticket? 'Cause if it has, it can have your ship.

Beat.

Where did you go?

Ricky   Bear Island.

Claxton   Three thousand fucking mile there and three thousand fucking mile back. For less than five hundred kit of cod. I could've caught more than that in Pickie Park boating lake with a fucking magnet.

Ricky   I lost a couple of days. We snagged a set of gear.

Claxton   How the fuck do you lose gear at Bear Island, it's a fucking beach?!

Ricky   Be a wreck, I guess.

Claxton   This isn't a guessing game. Did you look at the fucking charts? No! You were following the bloke in front, you lazy bastard.

Ricky   I know why you're doing this.

Claxton   Now, I thought you'd think that. Which is why I gave you an hour sitting outside my office to think about that possibility. And, I'm absolutely certain, with this haul you'll have come to the conclusion that there is nothing personal in this whatsoever, but it all comes down to an entirely rational business decision that Ricky Toov is neither use nor ornament.

Ricky   Are you putting me on walkabout?

Claxton   If you were me, you'd put yourself on walkabout.

Ricky   I did think about it, for an hour, and I still think it's personal.

Claxton   I could take you to court, for negligence, losing a set of gear, and you'd be ruined for life. Of course, I'm glad you've fucked up, you know, in the job, like a hundred skippers before you because if I'd sacked you when I wanted to sack you everyone would've said that Donald Claxton had no reason to sack Ricky Toov, it's just personal.

Ricky   You bastard.

Silence.

Claxton   No! That is the point. If you were a trawler owner, and one of your skippers came back from the Arctic with nothing worth talking about but an halibut as big as Tommy Cooper, what would you do?

Ricky   I'm not a trawler owner am I, and I never fucking will be.

Claxton   The answer is, you'd sack him.

Ricky   I haven't slept for three weeks trying to catch fish for you.

Claxton   If you're looking for sympathy you'll find it in the dictionary between shit and syphilis. Leave your log on the chart table.

He turns his back. **Ricky** *just stands there for a few seconds, and then turns to the chart table where there is a large stone paper weight holding down a chart. He puts his log on the table and sees the paper weight which attracts him. He doesn't touch it.*

Claxton   There's a paper weight on that chart table. You could smash a man's brains in whilst he had his back turned.

Ricky   I'm sorry what happened that night in London, but it, and it sounds barmy this, and I can't explain why, really, but it was none of my doing.

The two men are still for a few seconds, and then **Ricky** *leaves, closing the door behind him. The phone beeper goes, it's* **Charlotte***.*

Charlotte   A link call, Wick Radio. The *Rider Haggard*.

Claxton   Yes.

Wick Radio (*voiceover/Scottish accent*)   Wick Radio here. I have the FV *Rider Haggard* call sign Golf Bravo November on the RT. I can patch him in and make a link call? All link calls charged to the ship in gold francs.

Claxton   Wick Radio, hello, yes, we will take the call.

The call is patched in, so increase in distort.

Pops (*voiceover*)   Percy?

Claxton   Donald Claxton here, what can I do for you, skipper?

Pops   Oh, I wanted Percy.

Claxton   He's not here. This is your last chance, what do you want?

Pops   I need a new bosun. Can you fly one out please, Mr Claxton? I've only just got here. Spitzbergen.

Claxton   What happened to the old one?

Silence.

Skipper, you were going to tell Percy, so why can't you tell me?

Pops   Oh bloody hell, alright. Al Dacre, Alan Dacre, last week, steaming out, he'd asked me to set him off at Aberdeen 'cause last time he was home, he found out his lass was having an affair with a fellah from Skidby, a stump grinder, and he wanted to go back to Hull and catch 'em, you know . . .

Claxton   – *in flagrante delicto.*

Pops   Does that mean 'on the job'?

Laughter from Wick Radio.

Claxton   Yes. They're all laughing at you on the RT.

Pops   Aye, I bet, so I says no fucking way. Anyhow, this morning he kicks me cabin door in and attacks me with a bottle. He's obviously hammered. We had a big fight and I just grabbed him round the neck and he was bucking away around the cabin and if I'd had a sombrero in mi hand I coulda won the rodeo. He was tryna kill me so I had no choice, I jumped on his chest and brok' an arm and two of his ribs.

Claxton   Did that shut him up?

Pops   It did, that's the good news, but the bad news is, he's got two broken ribs, and a broken arm which needs setting.

Claxton   What do you want me to do? I'm in Hull.

Pops   I know, I know. Can I put him off in Vardo?

Claxton   What longitude are you?

Pops   35. Vardo pretty much due south. But it'll take two days steaming.

Claxton   What if you steamed west, to Honnigsvag?

Pops   That'll take me three days. Honnigsvag is 10 degrees west.

Claxton   Yes, but it's good fishing all the way to the hospital.

Pops   Ha, ha, ha.

Claxton   Seriously, is he gonna die?

Pops   Of a broken heart he might, yeah.

Claxton   Exactly.

Pops   Who's ever died of a broken heart, eh?

Claxton *ponders this.*

Pops   Hello?

Claxton   I'm here.

Pops   What is a stump grinder?

Claxton   Someone who grinds stumps.

Pops   I can't picture it.

Enter **Lizzie Jopling**. *A woman of about forty. She looks determined. She is dressed in a coat over fish-filleting clothing and white welly boots.* **Charlotte** *follows her in, flustered.*

Claxton   Forestry. Don't let it bother you. Is that all?

Pops   Yeah. I'll sign off. Wick Radio, I'm signing off. Golf Bravo Nov –

Claxton *hangs up the phone.*

Charlotte   I'm sorry, sir.

Lizzie   I'm not!

Charlotte   This is Mrs Jopling. Jack Jopling's wife. I told her –

Claxton   – that's alright, Charlotte. Come in, Mrs Jopling. Have you finished the list?

Charlotte   Yes. But the vicar's not –

Claxton   – I'll look out for the vicar. Bring it in, and then you can go home.

Charlotte   Thanks.

She leaves.

Claxton   Sit down, Mrs Jopling.

Lizzie *sits.* **Claxton***'s chair is significantly higher than hers.*

Lizzie   Bit low down here.

Claxton *lowers his chair. It's comedically slow hydraulics.*

Claxton   Is that better?

Lizzie   Ha! Do you do that all the time?

Claxton   Never done it before. Just did it for you.

Lizzie   Ha! I didn't come here to laugh.

Charlotte *enters with the list in her hand which she leaves on the chart table.*

Charlotte   I'll clock off now.

Claxton   See you tomorrow. Thank you.

Lizzie   Tarra, love.

Charlotte *shoots a glance at* **Lizzie***, leaves and closes the door behind her.* **Claxton** *stands and puts the kettle on.*

Claxton   Tea, Mrs Jopling?

Lizzie   I an't come here to drink tea.

Claxton   Do you mind if I have one?

Lizzie   If you consider drinking tea more important than listening to me, then go ahead, and then you'll have to put up with me thinking badly of you.

Claxton   You think badly of me already.

Continuing making tea by putting a tea bag into a tea pot.

Lizzie   Don't you warm the pot first?

Claxton   No.

Lizzie   Why am I not surprised.

Claxton   You've lost me now.

Lizzie   Cutting corners. Again.

Claxton   All our ships are Lloyd's Grade 1 and Board of Trade approved. Fifteen men have lost their lives. I have asked myself searching questions about whether I have done all I can do – safety, equipment, whatever. On this occasion I'm afraid, it is once again, nature, the weather, the sea. It's hell, but I have to keep going.

Lizzie   My heart's bleeding for you.

Claxton   I often wonder if that is the job, my real job, in this industry – to be hated. The work isn't taking the financial risks and investing in new trawlers and better gear in order to provide jobs for the whole of West Hull, but, like a Guy on Guy Fawkes night, the job is to be the focus of a community's hatred.

Lizzie   It's dead easy to blame the weather, but why are you fishing off Iceland in February in the fost place?

Claxton   Because the cod go there for their holidays.

Lizzie   I don't like your tone. Mekking jokes. Look at all the 1968 sinkings, three of them, all in February, all iced up. You can have as much safety gear in the world but you an't gorra chance in February. I know how this industry works, I did feudalism at school. Our lads are just cannon fodder.

Claxton   So, what do we do, West Hull, we all take February off, go to Barbados?

Lizzie   Again. Joking! Don't get sarcastic with me.

Claxton   For every day that one of my trawlers is in dock I'm losing three thousand pounds. I'd go out of business if they didn't go out to Iceland in February. And how would you get through the month without an income?

Lizzie   I have me own money. From work.

Claxton   The men need work.

Lizzie   I said, when I had our Philip, I said he's not going to sea, if it's the last thing I do, and I told him. But your ship's runner whatshisname –

Claxton   – Percy

Lizzie   That's him, he signed our Philip on.

Claxton   As deckie learner?

Lizzie   Yeah. I don't get a day's peace, knowing he's out there.

Claxton   Which ship is he on?

Lizzie   The *George Eliot*.

Claxton   He's with a good skipper then.

Lizzie   Percy originally signed him on the *Virginia Woolf* but I wasn't having that.

Claxton   Why not?

Lizzie   You don't name a ship after a woman. It's unlucky.

Claxton   *George Eliot . . .*

Lizzie   – what?

Claxton   Nothing.

Lizzie   The *Graham Greene*, there's another one. Green's unlucky. Why tempt fate. I don't believe in any of it, I'm not superspicious but, you know, it dun't cost owt either does it.

Claxton   The *George Eliot* has set off back.

Lizzie   Has it?

Claxton   Yes.

Lizzie   He's out of this weather then? Away from Iceland then?

Claxton   Yes.

She visibly relaxes, like the air in her body is sucked out.

They'll dock on Thursday. Be the only ship to land. He'll pick up a healthy lot of cash.

Lizzie   Money! The root of it all.

Claxton   And your husband, Jack Jopling –

Lizzie   – sod him!

Claxton   OK? He's one of the survivors of the *Graham Greene*. So maybe green was lucky for him.

Lizzie   Our Philip promised me he was going to tech college to train as a chef. Every day, every day, I'm at top pitch, worrying.

She gets a hanky out.

Claxton   But your son was attracted to fishing presumably by its feudal structure, and dangerous working conditions.

Lizzie   There you go again, getting sarcy.

Claxton   Yes, that was sarcastic. I apologise. But men lie for what they love.

Lizzie   How the bloody hell does he know he loves fishing when he's never been?!

Claxton   They say fishing is in the blood, but, of course, that's nonsense, but it is in the culture.

Lizzie   What culture? Hessle Road has no culture.

Claxton   Young men see the deckies come home, in the pubs, their pockets stuffed with money, three days off, taxis –

Lizzie   – three-day millionaires.

Claxton   Bespoke tailoring. They look like rock stars. They get the girls. Jack got you.

Lizzie   I don't know how. I didn't even like him back then.

Claxton   You didn't even like Jack when you first met him?

She drops her head. A kind of shame.

Lizzie   I'm not here for Jack. I'm here for my son.

Claxton   Iceland might give you Philip back for good.

Lizzie   How do you mean?

Claxton   The Athling vote next week –

Lizzie   – what's that? Their parliament?

Claxton   Yes. They want to extend to two hundred miles.

Lizzie   I hope they do. Put an end to all this madness.

Claxton   And me out of business.

Lizzie   Good. This is no way to live. Will that be another cod war then?

Claxton   Probably.

Lizzie   And we always lose them.

Claxton   Indeed we do.

Lizzie   Why do we lose?

Claxton   Everyone in Europe recognises that Iceland needs the cod more than we do.

Lizzie   I've heard Icelanders don't eat cod.

Claxton   They do eat cod but they have a saying 'we don't eat cod because we don't eat money'. Demersals are their only means of foreign exchange.

Lizzie   How did you vote?

Claxton   Vote?

Lizzie   In the Europe referendum?

Claxton   Ah.

Lizzie   You've got to be 'No, get out' aren't you?

Claxton   I voted 'yes' to stay in.

Lizzie   You, a trawler owner, voted to stay in the Common Market and let them have our fish?

Claxton   We're a distant water fleet. We don't fish British waters, there's not enough fish in the North Sea to keep me going.

Lizzie   And it's not as if Belgium's got any rich fishing grounds is it?

Claxton   I voted 'yes' so I can sell my fish products to Europe.

Lizzie   You're a capitalist?

Claxton   Guilty. How did you vote?

Lizzie   'Out'.

Claxton   Because you're an anti-capitalist?

Lizzie   I'm Labour aren't I and I listen to Tony Benn.

Claxton   And Enoch Powell?

Lizzie   I didn't listen to him. Anyhow you and your lot won, you got what you wanted.

Claxton   67 per cent, to 33 per cent. That's a massive win, not just capitalists.

Lizzie   I've always been on the losing side. If it wasn't for bad luck, I wouldn't have no luck at all.

Claxton   B.B. King. No! Albert King.

Lizzie   Aye, well, he nicked it off my Uncle Les.

Claxton   The Common Market won't damage us but Iceland could kill us off. You'll lose your job.

Lizzie   When do they vote?

Claxton   Next week.

Lizzie   West Hull?

Claxton   It's all fish and fish trades. Maybe Jack will get a shore job.

Lizzie   I'm not having that. That wouldn't work.

Claxton   No?

Lizzie   He'll be home every night, won't he.

Claxton   You don't want your husband home every night?

Lizzie   Do you know him?

Claxton   I know the skippers, not the men.

Lizzie *is struggling.*

Lizzie   He's a bastard. A nasty bastard.

Silence.

I hoped, when I heard, I hoped.

She doesn't cry but she puts her head in her hands and pulls her head down to her knees in grief. **Claxton** *is a bit hopeless. He stands, shocked, not knowing what to do.*

I was hoping he'd died.

Claxton   Can I get you a glass of water? Whisky?

Lizzie   Whisky!

Claxton *prepares to pour a glass.*

Lizzie   I went to the church. Me! And I don't believe in God. I sat in there and prayed for him to be dead.

He gives her the glass of whisky.

Thanks.

She drinks it down in one like a hard drinker.

Claxton   Give me your glass.

She gives him the glass. Their hands touch. They both react by looking at each other.

Sorry.

He refills her glass and gives it back to her.

Do you mind if I join you?

Lizzie   You don't have to ask.

He pours himself one.

Don't believe this. Me, sitting in here, crying, drinking your whisky.

Claxton   You were in the Bethel, though you don't believe in God, you were praying that Jack was one of those lost.

Lizzie   I felt evil, but at the same time I thought if there is a God and He knows everything, then He'll know what Jack's done to me and He'll know I'm not evil, I just want a life without all his selfish bastard wickedness. Sorry. Am I evil? Is that evil?

Claxton   I don't think I'm qualified to judge. Why don't you do what I did?

Lizzie   Divorce?

Claxton   You could leave Jack.

Lizzie   On them three days when he's home I go to my mother's. It's alright innit usually. When he's fishing, he's away for three weeks, and the house is mine. Every month I have three weeks to myself and I get out the way when he's home.

Claxton   You'd need a divorce if we all took February off.

Lizzie (*laughing*)   Ha, ha! Yes. You're right.

She's recovered.

Claxton   Cigarette?

Lizzie   I will, ta.

He offers her a cigarette from a silver case, and lights it for her. She takes a drag. He takes one for himself. Lights it.

Oh bugger, I've made a fool of myself. Again.

Claxton   No, no, no.

Lizzie   Thought you'd be cigars. Big money man.

Claxton   I started smoking tabs when in the army. 1956. Rhineland. Tanks.

Lizzie   Did you enjoy it?

Claxton   Tearing over German crops in peacetime in a three-ton tank?

Lizzie   Ha, ha! You loved it?!

Claxton   I can't protect your Philip any more than any other man.

Lizzie   William Wilberforce was a Hull man. He wouldn't like it.

Claxton   Fishing is not slavery. The men are free agents.

Lizzie   Casual. Disposable.

Claxton   That's how they like it. Where do you work? Fish filleting?

Lizzie   I'm on the evening shift at Waudby's. Six to ten.

Claxton   You're gonna be late.

She stands.

No, no, no. Sit down. I know Willy Waudby.

He picks the phone up, flicks through a Rolodex, and dials a number.

How long have you worked there?

Lizzie   Over ten year.

Claxton (*on the phone*)   Could I speak to Mister Waudby please? . . . Inland Revenue inspectors . . . (*He winks to* **Lizzie**.) . . . Willy! . . . Very good. I've got one of your back shift filleters here, Lizzie Jopling . . . her Jack was on the *Graham Greene* . . . yes, he did survive, but there was some confusion over whether he had or not, and Lizzie is still in shock . . . so you'll not sack her for missing a shift then? . . . The night off, on full pay . . . good, because I think she's been working on the assumption that you're a heartless bastard. Ha, ha! . . . Alright. Goodbye!

Phone down.

Lizzie   The shift off on full pay? Bloody hell.

Claxton   Urgent domestic stress. His phrase.

Lizzie   Ta. For that. Have you got an ashtray?

Claxton *produces an ashtray which they both use, one after the other.*

Lizzie   You know, you don't seem to be as big a bastard as everyone says.

Claxton   What do they say?

Lizzie   That you don't give a shit for the men. That you live for your shooting, and golf, and all that posh Beverley set.

Claxton   I don't play golf.

They both lean in at the same time to dot their cigarettes.

Lizzie   I can't look at an ashtray without . . .

Claxton   – without what?

Lizzie   It's a funny kind of sharing innit.

Claxton   The intimacy of the ashtray?

Lizzie   Yeah. I first met Jack, I was singing in Subway Club, I used to do Patsy Cline covers. My favourite was 'Three cigarettes in an ashtray'.

Claxton   I thought it was 'Two cigarettes in an ashtray'.

Lizzie   No, but that is the first line.

(Sings.)
    Two cigarettes in an ashtray.

Patsy Cline and her lover, that's two cigarettes –

Claxton   – the happy couple.

Lizzie   – yes, but then someone new comes along.

Claxton   A man or a woman?

Lizzie   A woman.

Claxton   And this new woman, is she a smoker?

Lizzie   Yes! Of course she is!

Claxton   Or there wouldn't be a song!

Lizzie   The ashtray now has three cigarettes –

Claxton   – getting crowded, an odd number, disconcerting, threat, pain –

Lizzie   – and then, at the end, for the final verse, there's only one cigarette in the ashtray.

Claxton   Whose cigarette is that?

Lizzie   Patsy Cline's! It has to be Patsy Cline's.

Claxton   Not if the stranger was her lesbian lover. The last cigarette would be her abandoned fellah's.

Lizzie   Ha! It's Patsy Cline's. She's the one left.

Claxton   And what does she do then?

Lizzie   She watches her cigarette burn away.

Claxton   Her life . . .

Lizzie   I wanted him dead. And then I could start again.

Claxton   He doesn't have to die for that to happen.

Lizzie   No. He dunt.

She stands and dots her cigarette. She's intent on going.

And I came here to give you a bollocking.

Claxton   But instead of that you discovered that the trawler owner is a human being. That's got to be time well spent hasn't it.

Lizzie   Aye. I guess.

Claxton   Do you still sing?

Lizzie   Yeah. I do the clubs. But I write my own songs too.

Claxton   Ah! Excellent.

Lizzie   The clubs round here only want covers.

Claxton   Go to art college. All the pop groups start at art college.

Lizzie (*surprised*)   Why did you say that?

Claxton   What?

Lizzie   Art college?

Claxton   Because it's true. David Bowie, Keith Richards –

Lizzie   They wouldn't take me.

Claxton   Why not?

Lizzie   I'm a fish wife!

Claxton   Not for much longer. How old are you?

Lizzie   Bloody hell. I'm not saying.

Claxton   Philip's sixteen? You'll have had him at –

Lizzie   – I'm thirty-three. I look older. It's the wellies.

Claxton   I can imagine.

Lizzie   What can you imagine?

Claxton   I can imagine an art school wanting someone like you, to, I don't know, broaden their intake. Can you draw?

Lizzie   Course. Got an 'O' level.

Claxton   There you go then. The council would give you a grant.

Lizzie   Would they?

Claxton   Have you ever had an education grant?

Lizzie   Don't be daft.

Claxton   They can't refuse you, if you get in. Go to London. Get away from Jack.

There is a knock and the door opens. **Reverend Wallace Polkinghorne** *comes in, dog collar showing over slightly hippy clothes.*

Wallace   Sorry!

Claxton   Wallace, can you give me two minutes?

Wallace   I'll wait out here.

He closes the door.

Claxton   It's the vicar.

Lizzie   At every carcass a vulture.

Claxton   Bit unfair.

Lizzie *stands.*

Lizzie   Thanks for the whisky. That's me done for the day.

Claxton   Are you singing tonight?

Lizzie   No. Did you want to come?

Claxton   I didn't mean . . . I worried when you said, 'That's me done for the day.' I was worried that you had a booking that you might have to cancel.

Lizzie   I don't.

Claxton   But you said, 'Did you want to come?'

Lizzie   Would you like to come?

Claxton   You do have a show tonight!

Lizzie   Not tonight. Saturday I'm playing Stevedores and Dockers in the Old Town.

Claxton   I can't go there.

Lizzie   No. Of course not. Sunday . . . Old Goole WMC.

Silence.

I didn't tell you. It's in the paper. I'm not inviting you.

Claxton   OK. So, I know where you are on Sunday.

Lizzie   It's a members' club so I'll have to bona fide you in. Talk to Gareth on the door. Oh my God!

Claxton   Don't worry. It's Goole. It's not Hull. No one knows me.

Lizzie   What I said before, you know . . . about Jack –

Claxton   – everything's confidential.

Lizzie   Tarra. Oh my God. I can't believe it.

She opens the door, looks at him without smiling and leaves, closing the door. **Claxton** *contemplates the ashtray and its two stubs. He clears it away. He turns the lights off again and watches* **Lizzie** *walk along the dock. He turns the lights back on and opens the door.*

Claxton   Vicar. Do I call you vicar?

Wallace *enters.*

Wallace   Wallace.

Claxton   Welcome to Hull.

Wallace   They told me before I chose Hessle Road.

Claxton   Told you what?

Wallace   That West Hull is the second most pagan parish in Britain.

Claxton   What's the first?

Wallace   East Hull.

Claxton   God doesn't seem to notice or care about Hull. Why would anyone believe?

Wallace   Jesus was a fisherman.

Claxton   Not off Iceland.

Wallace (*offering his hand*)   Wallace Polkinghorne.

Claxton (*shaking hands*)   Donald Claxton. Polkinghorne. That's a great name. Cornwall?

Wallace   Yes! Though my people had moved along to Devon by the time I came along.

Claxton   There you go then, there's your connection, your way in, for them.

Wallace   How do you mean?

Claxton   A lot of these fishing families in Hull have Devon roots. The Devon families invested in the North Sea and built up fleets of smacks sailing out of Hull.

Wallace   Excellent. They might accept me then.

Claxton   I wouldn't bank on it. I've had a list typed up for you.

He gives him the papers from the chart table.

Wallace   Yes, good, this is what I need.

Claxton   Tea, coffee?

Wallace   Coffee please, maybe not, I've had about six today. I'm buzzing.

Claxton   We have a defibrillator.

Wallace   Ha!

Claxton   I'm on whisky?

Wallace   Ooh! Yes please.

Claxton *prepares two whiskies.*

Claxton   I can't offer you ice. Ironic. I spend six thousand pounds a month on ice but I don't have any in the office, sorry. I could go on the dock, but I might get pushed in.

Wallace   Really?

Claxton   Of course not. Tough time to start work in a new parish.

Wallace   I can't think about my bad luck.

Claxton   Of course.

Whisky handed over.

Thank you.

Wallace *takes a decent shot of whisky.*

Wallace Grrrrr! Smashing.

Claxton Do you have a date for the memorial yet?

Wallace I wanted to discuss that with you.

Claxton Holy Trinity. Massive, and the place will be packed.

Wallace Good.

Claxton Not with believers though, with mourners.

Wallace Would you read? I could choose something for you.

Claxton No, no, no. We go, we go along, but we don't like to attract attention.

Wallace Is this . . . I presume you took over from your father?

Claxton Yes. He lost six ships in forty years. This is my first. Or, rather, strictly my second. I lost the *Walter Scott*, what, eight years ago, broke up on rocks off Stonehaven, on the way back from Bear Island. A full fish room too. Not that any of us cared about that. But Dad was still around, not running anything, but always on the dock, you know, he knew everyone, so he did the widows' walk.

Wallace I've heard about the walk.

Claxton I do it tomorrow. Though widows doesn't seem like the right word for these girls. Some of them are eighteen or nineteen if that.

Wallace Sounds rather penitential. Self-flagellation?

Caxton You're the holy man. You go in the first house, and they give you a cup of tea, and, ironically, you always sit in the dead man's chair, by the fire. It's always winter, because that's when you lose the ships. You offer your polite commiserations, give the girl, the letter, and his wages for that trip, say your goodbyes and out into the street again and the gaze of everyone, the dockers, retired trawlermen, grandmas and granddads, who are silent, never any abuse, but they're there, and the tables have turned, they're commanding, and for once in their lives they're in control of you. Making you do the walk. And you walk to the next house, and the next, and the next. The walk, in the old days would take about six hours – twenty widows pretty much all down the one road, Hessle Road, and the skipper's wife in Hessle village. But this one, for me, tomorrow, everything will be different.

Wallace   What's changed?

Claxton   In the last six years Hull council knocked down all the slum housing down Hessle Road and moved the families out to the new estates, so I have fifteen widows, with only six on Hessle Road, then two on Orchard Park, two more on Bransholme, two in Sutton and three on Bilton Grange.

That's like thirty or forty miles walking.

Wallace   Shall I accompany you?

Claxton   No, no, no! You can't break tradition.

Wallace   I'll be with you in spirit. And the memorial needs to be after the walk obviously?

Claxton   That would be clever.

Wallace   You write individual letters?

Claxton   By hand, not typed. I try and make each one different, personal. Percy, the ship's runner, tells me about each man –

Wallace   – something esoteric. That's the trick.

Claxton   I feel like a fraud. I know the skippers a bit, not too much because I have to sack them every now and then, standards, fear keeps them on their toes, but I don't know the crew. And I don't want to. So each letter of heartfelt condolence is complete bollocks.

Wallace   Your motivation is good. To express your love.

Claxton   It's not love though is it.

Wallace   I believe it is. 'The kelson of creation is love.'

Claxton   Walt Whitman.

Wallace   Yes?!

Claxton   I read English at Cambridge. I liked Whitman.

Wallace   *Leaves of Grass* is an extraordinary insightful –

Claxton   – the Bible not good enough for you? Do you believe in heaven and hell? Or are you one of these trendy vicars that thinks God could be a piece of bacon rind?

Wallace   Jesus, for me, was one of three things. A madman, a clever conman, or the son of God. I incline to the latter.

Claxton   You'd be out of a job with madman or conman.

Wallace   Whitman is often considered to be atheist, but that is an incorrect reading.

Claxton   What was he then?

Wallace   He believed in immanence, the idea that God is in everything.

Claxton   So God is a piece of bacon rind!

Wallace   *In* a piece of bacon rind, yes.

Claxton   Maple smoked, my preference. They say you're a communist.

Wallace   God and communism. Unlikely bed fellows.

Claxton   The memorial service gives you a problem.

Wallace   Yes?

Claxton   'For those in peril on the sea'.

Wallace   'Eternal Father, Strong to Save'? A beautiful hymn.

Claxton   Half of them will sing it, and half of them will walk out.

Wallace   Oh dear.

Claxton   Makes dying at sea sound like something noble, patriotic. Whereas they know that their husband, son or father has died for one half of a fish and chip supper.

Wallace   We don't need to include it.

Claxton   But if you don't include it, they'll want to know why not. Basically, you can't win.

Wallace   The reason I've got Whitman on my mind is that he's very good on death. May I? I wondered . . . well, let me know what you think.

He takes a copy of Leaves of Grass *from his pocket and opens it at a marked page.*

What do you think has become of the young and old men?
And what do you think has become of the women and children?
All goes onward and outward, nothing collapses,
And to die is different from what any one supposed, and luckier.
Has any one supposed it lucky to be born?
I hasten to inform him or her it is just as lucky to die, and I know it.

Claxton   You wouldn't get out alive.

Wallace   Oh. I thought it was rather good.

Claxton   It is, but it's dangerous.

Wallace   Play safe.

Claxton   Can I ask . . . do you . . . are you confident in defining, explaining evil?

Wallace   Go on.

Claxton   Is a wife evil for wishing her husband dead?

Wallace   I would say that depends.

Claxton   On what?

Wallace   Whether his evil is the . . . seminal evil.

Claxton   Seminal, as in he was evil before she was evil?

Wallace   There's plenty of selfishness, bad behaviour, which is not evil.

Claxton   So she's not evil if she wishes an evil bastard dead, but she is evil if she wishes a selfish bastard dead.

Wallace   Y . . . up. If one believes in God.

Claxton   Which takes us back to bacon rinds.

Wallace   If not God, what do they believe in?

Claxton   Fate. None of them can swim. Just prolongs the agony. Fate, Old Father Neptune.

Wallace   It's a strong community though.

Claxton   Maybe the answer is they believe in 'each other'.

Wallace   Would it help if I did a trip? On a trawler. To find out . . . to understand a little more.

Claxton   It's three weeks.

Wallace   I know that. I was told.

Claxton   It is the kind of thing Walt Whitman would do.

Wallace   Why three weeks?

Claxton   We go to the Arctic, that's three days to get there and three days to get back and a couple of weeks fishing. Greenland, Iceland, Barents Sea.

Wallace   How long between trips?

Claxton   Three days.

Wallace   Only three days rest and sleep?

Claxton   And drinking.

Wallace   I like a drink.

During the next **Claxton** *tops up the glasses. Maybe opens a new bottle of whisky.*

Claxton   Let me try and explain how this industry works, from my perspective. One day, two years ago, when I was stone cold sober, I went to see the bank manager, who is, by reputation, teetotal. I begged him to lend me two hundred thousand pounds to build a big sidewinder trawler that might refresh the fleet. Reluctantly he agreed, and the following day I visited Hemming and Clyde, maritime architects, both of whom, as far as I could tell, hadn't been drinking. They created this brilliant design, and then, after a glass of home-made lemonade I chose Cook, Welton and Gemmel to build the ship, partly because their highly qualified engineers work within the confines of a *dry* dock. A year later the ship is built and ready for its first trip. So far so good, and I'm a happy man, full of hope. And then I ask Percy, my ship's runner, to find me a crew. He scrapes together twenty kids off Hessle Road. And I mean kids, the skipper is likely to be twenty-five, if I'm lucky. And when they arrive at the lock pit at two o'clock in the morning to catch the tide, to begin work, in this brand new state-of-the-art fish-catching machine, in what is, without question, the most dangerous job there has ever been since regimental flag bearer at the Somme, when they turn up, each one of these kids is totally, utterly, shitfaced pissed. Cheers!

Wallace   Cheers!

They down their whisky.

The survivors, where are they now?

Claxton   Reykjavik. Five of them. They're coming back on the *Daniel Defoe*. Which has been fishing off Spitzbergen. I've got her to go into Reykjavik to pick them up.

Wallace   Could you go out there and join them?

Claxton   Why?

Wallace   There must be issues.

Claxton   The last thing the survivors want is me turning up.

Wallace   I mean medical bills, and hotels, and I don't know
. . . you could ease the situation. Maybe fly them home,
rather than asking them to go back into a trawler for three
days. A gift.

Claxton (*beat*)   When can Holy Trinity host the memorial?

Wallace   Everything is pointing to Wednesday next week.
Does that work for you?

Claxton   Perfect.

Wallace   I'll try and write something then.

Claxton   If you want that 'something esoteric' on each man,
come in and see Percy. He'll be in tomorrow.

Wallace   Excellent. I will.

They both stand. Silence.

Claxton   Would you like to hear the skipper's last
transmission?

Wallace   There is such a thing?

Claxton   He was in touch with Wick Radio. He was
dodging to the end –

Wallace   – dodging?

Claxton   Head to wind and dodging. Holding the ship
straight into the wind, trying to avoid a broadside. He was
on the radio as he was doing it.

He sets up the tape recorder, putting a spool tape in the player.

Everyone called him Stabba, it wasn't his name, he was called
Jim, but he had a nick name 'Stabbasausage', kind of a
catchphrase.

Wallace   Stabbasausage? How colourful.

Claxton   Instead of swearing, I think. Maybe quite a moral man.

The tape plays.

Wick Radio (*distort*)   Wick Radio, Wick Radio, Wick Radio, the ships using this frequency, the ships on this frequency, will you keep off please, you're interfering with a distress.

Stabba (*distort and matter of factly, no panic*)   She's heeling over now . . . listing very badly . . . she's lain over . . . I can't get her back . . . engines on full . . . help me . . . she's going over, she's going over, we're going over . . . give my love and the crew's love to the wives and families.

All that remains on the tape is a whine. **Wallace** *sits involuntarily.* **Claxton** *stops the tape.*

Wallace   Good God. Good Lord. 'Give our love to the wives and families.' Extraordinary.

Claxton   That's what they believe in.

Wallace   Family?

Claxton   Maybe that's all there is.

He turns the tape off.

End of Act.

Reykjavik

February 1976. Reykjavik. Evening. **Jack, Snacker** *and* **Baggie**
sit drinking in the bar area of the hotel lobby. They all wear clothes
they haven't chosen, clothes given to them by a local Reykjavik
charity. These clothes are recognisably Icelandic, specifically the
jumpers. **Snacker** *wears trousers that are too small.* **Jack** *wears*
trousers that are too big – he has folded the waist band of his
trousers over on itself and tucked the jumper into the trousers to try
and keep them up. **Baggie** *is the only one that looks comfortable in*
the charity clothes. **Snacker** *has a bandage around his head;* **Jack**
has the middle finger of his right hand bandaged; **Baggie** *is*
seemingly unscathed. Before them are pint glasses, and empty
bottles of non-alcoholic pilsner and empty bottles of Brennivin.
Einhildur, *a young Icelander, is behind the bar. A storm rages*
outside. A ship's horn sounds in the harbour, long and mournful.

Jack (*standing*) Baggie! 'nother one?

Baggie No, bit early for me.

Jack No, no, no. Shurrup, you're having another one.

Baggie I don't want one.

Jack I aren't drinking on mi fucking tod.

Einhildur *looks up.*

Baggie Stop swearing.

Jack Fizz is dead.

Baggie Aye.

Jack Like a brother to me. And I'm gonna lose a finger
tomorrow! So . . . I'll swear as much as I fucking like!

He stands to make the point.

Not just any finger, my fucking all-time favourite finger.

Baggie   Aye, but remember, we're in Reykjavik. You're an ambassador. For Hull.

The phone behind the bar rings. **Einhildur** *answers it.*

Baggie   We're all ambassadors for Hull at all times.

Einhildur (*from behind the bar*)   Mister Bagnal?

Jack   That's him.

Einhildur   Your wife is on the phone from Hull, England.

Baggie   Ta, love.

He goes up to the bar.

Jack   Eh, Snack. She's a bit of alright.

Baggie (*on the phone*)   Aye.

Jack   Looks like she runs this place on her tod.

Baggie (*on the phone*)   Aye.

Jack   Snacker?! Wake up, you little twat!

Baggie (*on the phone*)   Aye.

Jack *knuckles his head, and he wakes.*

Snacker   'kin'ell! What?

Jack   Her.

Baggie (*on the phone*)   Aye.

Einhildur *glances over.*

Snacker   Who?

Jack   Her!

Baggie (*on the phone*)   Harry's dead, he died last night . . . aye.

Snacker *looks at* **Einhildur**, *she looks back.*

Jack   Same again?

Snacker   Yeah.

Baggie (*on the phone*)   Aye.

Jack   I'll see if she's gorr any chips.

He approaches the bar.

Baggie (*on the phone*)   Can you chuck some straw over the rhubarb patch.

Jack (*to* **Einhildur**)   Same again.

Baggie (*on the phone*)   . . . frost innit . . . ta, love . . . tarra . . .

He puts the phone down.

Jack   She had it yet?

Baggie   No. Week overdue now.

Jack   You'd expect that if it were her fost, but what's this one?

Baggie   Five.

Jack   Should just pop out.

Baggie   Aye.

Jack   Have you gorr any chips, love?

Einhildur   No.

Jack   No?

Einhildur   No.

Jack *and* **Baggie** *retreat to the table.*

Jack   I don't think she likes me.

Snacker   Why don't they have beer in Iceland?

Jack   'cause it's illegal.

Baggie   Temperance. Prohibition.

Snacker   Pro fucking what?

Baggie   Prohibition, the legal restriction of beer.

Snacker   So why do they sell this Brennivin?

Jack   Folks always have a need to clean their paint brushes.

Baggie   Brennivin's expensive so won't get drunk over much.

Snacker   But if it's all there is.

Baggie   Aye.

Jack   Will you stop saying 'aye'! We're from Hull, we're not fucking pirates.

Enter **Donald Claxton**. *He is dressed in his big camel-hair coat and a trilby with a scarf and gloves. The storm is briefly experienced.*

Jack   I know him.

Baggie   Donald Claxton . . . of Claxtons.

Jack   Fuck!

Claxton   Yes, fuck. I was told there were five survivors.

Baggie (*standing*)   Harry Thorpe died last night. I'm the bosun, Walter Bagnal, this is the third hand Jack Jopling, and this is Snacker, who's our snacker.

Claxton   That's you three, Harry, that's only four.

Snacker   Quayle.

Baggie   Michael Quayle isn't in this hotel.

Jack   He's not a survivor neither.

Claxton   He's alive?

Baggie   He is alive.

Claxton   Then in my book he's a survivor.

Jack   He gorr hissen put off in Helgafel two days afore your ship sank. That's a coward, not a survivor.

Claxton   I see.

Jack   You got no overnight bag?

Claxton   No. I went straight from the office to Heathrow. Beers?

Baggie   There is no beer, Mister Claxton.

Jack   You're in Iceland now.

Snacker   *Prohibition*, innit.

Jack   Buy a bottle of their Brennivin, and some of their no alcoholic beer –

Snacker   – pilsners.

Jack   Then we put the Brennivin, in the pilsners, and mek beer.

Claxton   And that's good is it?

Jack   No, it's fuckin' terrible.

Snacker   It's all we've got.

Claxton *goes off to the bar.*

Jack   What's that toff bastard doing out here?

Baggie   Dunno.

Jack   We could kill him.

Baggie   Idiot.

Jack   He's on his tod.

Snacker   Kill him? And then what?

Jack   Kill him again. What d'yer mean?

Snacker   The body.

Jack   Their fish dock's an' 'undred yards away.

Snacker   Fish dock? First place anyone would look. The best way, and this is a proven fact, the best way to dispose of a body is to feed it to pigs.

Jack   We're in a hotel in Reykjavik.

Snacker   Iceland must have a pig farm.

He stands, as if to move to **Einhildur***.*

Snacker   I'll ask her.

Jack   No! Sit down!

Baggie   Why d'yer wanna kill him?

Jack   He killed Fizz, my best china.

Baggie   He didn't kill Fizz, the ship sank.

Jack   Nick a knife from the kitchen.

Baggie   Jack, just shut it.

Jack   We're abroad. Bound to get away with it.

Baggie   No you wouldn't, you've told me.

Jack   You'd grass me would yer?

Baggie   Yes.

Jack   Alright. A finger then. Just one of his fingers. His fanny finger. His fucking frigging finger.

Snacker   Is he right-handed? He might be cack-handed?

Jack   One finger! That would square everything.

Baggie   Why?

Jack   'Cause I've heard he's the kind of bloke who wouldn't piss on your chips even if you was on fire.

Snacker   What?

Baggie   Either 'he *wouldn't* piss on you, if you were on fire'. Or 'he *would* piss on your chips'.

Jack   If you was on fire?

Baggie   No, he wouldn't even piss on you if you were on fire.

Snacker   To put you out.

Baggie   Because that would be a helpful thing to do. To piss on you.

Snacker   If you were on fire.

Jack   How does pissing on someone help?

Snacker   You're on fire!

Baggie   But pissing on your chips –

Snacker   – is malice.

Jack   What's malice?

Baggie   It's an unpleasant and not at all helpful thing to do.

Snacker   To piss on your chips.

Jack   If you're on fire?

Baggie   Let's start again. Pissing on you, if you was on fire, would be a kind and generous act.

Snacker   But he wouldn't do that.

Jack   Why not?

Snacker   Because he's the kind of bloke who'd piss on your chips.

Jack   So he would piss on mi chips, but he wouldn't piss on me?

Snacker   If you were on fire!

Baggie   Yes!

Jack   I think I've got it.

Snacker   He's charming my beautiful ears now.

Claxton *makes* **Einhldur** *laugh.*

Jack   Made her laugh. More than you have, Snack.

Snacker   Does she own this hotel, you think?

Jack   Na, she's nowt burr a lass.

Snacker   She's gorgeous.

Jack   Yer got a thing about ears have yer?

Snacker   Yeah. Hers are perfect.

He plays with his cards. **Claxton** *returns with a tray of drinks, with four bottles of pilsner and a bottle of Brennivin.*

Claxton   Cold in here.

Jack *holds up his bandaged finger.*

Jack   Cawld? That's fuckin' cawld.

Baggie   Frostbite.

Jack   They're gonna tek it off tomorrow.

Claxton   I'm sorry.

Jack *mixes the drinks.*

Jack   I've gorra question for you.

Claxton   I'm here to arrange getting you all back home –

Jack   – fuck that. Are you the kind of bloke who would piss on my chips? If they was on fire?

Baggie   Oh no.

Claxton   That would not be in my nature, to piss on anyone's chips.

Jack   Even if they was on fire?

Claxton   I wouldn't want to spoil them.

Baggie   But if *he* was on fire, Mister Claxton, you'd piss on him then wouldn't you?

Claxton   Without hesitation.

Jack (*stands aggressively*)   Why would you piss on me?!

Baggie   Sit down, Jack!

Claxton   I've flown to Iceland to do just that, metaphorically, piss on all your fires. Money, hospitals, hotels, get you back home.

Baggie   We appreciate it.

Claxton   You've got clothing.

Jack   I aren't going down Hessle Road in this get-up.

Snacker   The rescue fellah give us these.

Jack   When you sack a skipper, I've heard, you keep your back turned on 'em. Put him back on walkabout, never look him in the eye. Eh?

Claxton   If one of my skippers returns with an empty fish room he knows he'll be sacked.

Jack   But you could look 'em in the eye, couldn't you?

Claxton   There's pain for me when it happens. I've maybe lost fifty thousand pounds.

Baggie   Give him a break, Jack.

Beers are created and shared.

Claxton   Cheers!

Snacker   Cheers.

Claxton   Have you all had a chance to put a call in to your wives?

Baggie   Yes, sir.

Jack   Sir?

Snacker (*giggling*)   Jack hasn't.

Jack   The enemy? I'm not ringing her, she'd only chow at us.

Snacker   Is she the kind of woman who'd piss on your chips?

Jack   Our lass, she wouldn't piss on mi chips even if I was on fire!

Snacker   She would!

Baggie   *She would* piss on your chips.

Claxton   Your wife, Lizzie. I've met her.

Jack   Eh?

Claxton   She came into the office. Worried about, er . . . your Philip.

Jack   She wouldn't waste time worrying about me.

Claxton   Where did you meet her?

Jack   I'd sailed with Dillinger, and Dill knew the bloke what ran Subway Club, and he got her a job singing. She coulda been on the telly.

(*Sings.*)
   I'm crazy for feeling so lonely

Claxton   Patsy Cline.

Jack *stands and sings.*

Jack
   I'm crazy
   Crazy for feeling so blue
   I knew –

Baggie   Jack. That's enough. Sit down.

Snacker   They don't know Patsy Cline in Iceland.

Jack *sits.*

Claxton   She must be worried nonetheless.

Jack *stands and sings again.*

Jack
   Worry

Baggie   Jack!

Jack
Why do I let myself worry?
Wondering –

Einhildur *comes over.*

Einhildur   Please?! I have two guests back there in the restaurant.

Baggie   I'm so sorry.

Snacker   Hi. Do you work here?

Einhildur *looks at* **Snacker** *as if he's mad.* **Einhildur** *retreats to the bar.* **Jack** *sits.*

Jack   'Do you work here?'

Snacker   I know. Fuck!

Claxton   She's advertising a bar job in the window.

Jack   There you go, Snacker, yer in there.

Snacker *stands.*

Jack   Oi! Oi!

Snacker *sits.*

Snacker   Give me a minute.

Claxton (*to* **Jack**)   Has she stopped the singing? Your wife?

Jack   Yeah. Waudby's now, fish filleting, part-time. Pin money innit. It's her money, I don't know what she does with it.

Snacker   Buys pins.

Jack   Are you tekkin' the piss?

Baggie   And we're all the way back to piss.

Claxton   You said you'd sailed with Dillinger?

Jack   Aye, many a time.

Claxton   When my father was running the fleet, he was down the lock pit three o'clock one morning waiting for the tide and Dill rolls up with his mate, Lighthouse. Criterion had given them an old piano and –

Jack   – he bought it, they didn't give it him.

Claxton   Dad let him put it on board, and it sat there in the pounds for the whole three-week trip to Greenland. And he played it, while the lads were gutting, in the pounds, and sang.

Baggie   Must've been summer.

Claxton   Dillinger, eh? They broke the mould.

Silence.

Jack (*to* **Claxton**)   Eh, Mister Claxton –

Claxton   – Donald.

Jack   Donald. Did you know Ricky Toov fucked your missus?

Baggie (*head in hands*)   Oh.

Silence.

I'm so sorry, Mr Claxton.

Claxton   Jack, everybody in Hull knows that.

Jack   I know, but do you? You're not Hull, you're Pocklington. I was there that night.

Claxton   Silver Cod dinner, London. 1972.

Jack   That posh hotel on the Strand. The Saveloy.

Claxton   The Savoy.

Jack (*standing*)   Fucking Saveloy!

Baggie   Sit down, Jack! And shut up.

Claxton   Tell me something I don't know about my wife, Jack.

Jack   We put Ricky up to it. Yeah.

Claxton   A bet?

Jack   Not a bet, no, a kitty. Everyone on our table chucked in ten quid. Sixty quid. See if he could gerr off with her. Now, you didn't know that did you.

Baggie   I'm sorry, Mister Claxton.

Claxton   What were you doing there, Jack?

Jack   Me and Ricky was crew on the *St Crispin*, winning ship, Boyd Line. Now he was a fine fellah, Tom Boyd, different kind of trawler owner.

Snacker   How old was your wife, Mister Claxton? When Ricky fucked her. Sorry, just interested. Thirty, forty. 'Cause Ricky's young in't he.

Claxton   I know Ricky Toov, he's a beautiful man.

Jack   'kin'ell.

Claxton   I imagine he can have any woman he wants.

Jack   He can and he has.

Snacker   Have you forgiven her?

Baggie   Snacker! You can't –

Claxton   – I don't blame her, if that's what you mean, Snacker. It was not her fault. It is the human condition, to want what you can't have.

Snacker   She was bored with you. Is that what you mean?

Claxton   Do you have a girlfriend?

Jack   Two.

Claxton   Two women?

Jack   Double trouble. One's regular, and one's occasional. Like a table.

Claxton   And you asked out our Charlotte?

Jack   Your daughter?! Fuckin' hell, Snacker –

Claxton   – no, no. Charlotte is my clerk typist, in the office.

Snacker   Oh yeah. Her. Yeah. Nice ears.

Claxton   She was chuffed you survived.

Baggie   Chuffed, eh?

Jack   That's three women now, Snacker!

Snacker *stands.*

Snacker   Wish me luck.

He heads to the bar.

(*To* **Einhildur**.) Hi. (*Beat.*) Do you have a tray? I'll clear that table for you.

Einhildur *gives him a tray.*

Einhildur   Thank you.

Snacker *goes to the table with the tray and fills it with bottles and dead glasses.*

Claxton   Is there anything you need? Clothing. Medications?

Jack   Chips.

Claxton   You'd like some chips?

Baggie   They don't do chips in here.

Jack   Even though she has a restaurant.

Snacker   Let me ask her.

He goes up to the bar with the full tray.

Jack   That snacker of ours. He's not right, is he?

Snacker (*to* **Einhildur**)   There you go!

Einhildur   I appreciate that, thank you.

Snacker   Could you do us some chips please?

Einhildur   No, sorry. I am on my own.

Snacker   We're all alone. Aren't we. 'Cept Siamese twins. And you wouldn't wanna be one of them would yer.

He heads back to the table. **Einhildur** *goes through to the restaurant.*

Snacker   Beautiful ears, says 'no chips', she's on her tod.

Claxton (*brandishing cash*)   We'll see about that.

He stands and goes to the bar and, looking for **Einhildur**, *through to the restaurant.*

Baggie   Gonna chuck money at the problem. That's decent of him.

Jack   Fifteen men dead and he buys us a bag of chips?

Baggie   Why'd'yer bring up Ricky Toov?!

Jack   My finger, my fucking favourite fucking finger!

Baggie   He's come out here, he didn't have to.

Claxton *returns. In the background we see* **Einhildur** *put on a parka with hood and leave.*

Claxton   Einhildur's going to go out for chips.

Jack   Einhildur?

Snacker   You're a quick worker. We've been here two days and we don't know her name.

Claxton   So what happened? To the *Graham Greene.*

Baggie   Stabber couldn't get her out of a list.

Jack   Ice.

Baggie   Sidewinders are good sea ships –

Jack   – are they fuck!

Claxton   Is that what happened then?

Baggie   We were outside the fifty-mile limit, there's us, a couple of Scrob boats and a Ross sidewinder from Grimsby. I felt the wind change and before we knew it it's force nine or ten, we're iced up, and Stabba's put her head to wind. We're in two watches, below or cracking ice off the upperworks. I push these two, and Harry Thorpe, best man at my wedding –

Claxton   – I'm sorry.

Baggie   – into a raft and when she starts listing, I launched it. Thirty seconds later, you can't see anything, just hissing, and she was gone.

Jack   They're tekkin' mi finger off tomorrow.

Baggie   When's that new sidewinder of yours getting launched, Mister Claxton?

Claxton   Tomorrow, but I cancelled it. Didn't seem right.

Baggie   What's it to be called?

Claxton   The *Oscar Wilde*.

Jack   Bastard!

Claxton   Who? Me or Oscar Wilde?

Jack   You're both as bad as each other. The lads don't hate you 'cause you're rich, we all want to be rich; we don't hate you 'cause you're a cunt, Snacker's a cunt, aren't you, Snacker?

Snacker   Yeah.

Jack   And we like Snacker. You've not done the job. You've never done what we have to do. I knew this trip was doomed.

Claxton   How come?

Jack   I saw Michael Quayle at the lock pit.

Baggie   The lads don't like to sail with Quayle.

Snacker   Ha! Bonkers dreams he has!

Jack   Sick in the head.

Snacker   He's an entertainer!

Jack   He's unlucky.

Claxton   How can a man be unlucky? How can a man sink a ship?

Jack   Old Father Neptune's been nipping at his arse for fuckin' years.

Snacker   Michael knows when a ship is gonna sink.

Baggie   And he gets himself put off.

Jack   Is this the fost ship you've lost, Mister Claxton?

Claxton   Second. I lost the *Walter Scott* in 1968. Nineteen dead.

Baggie   So you've done two walks then?

Claxton   No, my father was, my father did the *Walter Scott* walk.

Jack   Why? You didn't have the balls for it.

Claxton   I should've done it.

Jack   But yer daddy wun't let yer?

Claxton   I was young, maybe too young.

Einhildur *arrives with chips. And puts them before* **Claxton,** *so they look like his chips.*

Einhildur   Your chips!

Claxton   *Takk*!

Einhildur *retreats with* **Snacker** *longing for her.* **Jack** *pours Brennivin over the chips.*

Baggie   What are you doing?!

Snacker   I was gonna eat them!

Jack *strikes a match or lighter and sets fire to them, and stands.*

Baggie   Jack?!

Jack   I lost a fucking finger!

Snacker   'kin'ell!

Jack   I'm gonna piss on your chips!

He whips his cock out. **Baggie** *dives on him and they fight, and roll on the floor.* **Snacker** *pours beer on the chips and puts the fire out.* **Claxton** *gets involved trying to separate* **Baggie** *and* **Jack**. **Jack** *punches* **Claxton**.

Claxton   You punched me?

Jack   And I'm gonna punch you again an'all.

Claxton *punches* **Jack** *and knocks him out.* **Einhildur** *comes over.*

Einhildur   Stop this! Mister Claxton! Who do you think you are!

Jack   We're fucking ambassadors!

Snacker   From Grimsby.

Enter **Michael Quayle**. *He is carrying a holdall, wearing a big overcoat and a baseball cap. He has his own clothes as he was put off rather than being shipwrecked.*

Baggie   Michael?

Claxton   Michael Quayle?

Quayle   Who the fuck are you?

Claxton   Donald Claxton.

Quayle   You don't look as big a cunt as they say. I need three of yers. Now! I've got Harry Thorpe in a box outside.

Baggie   His coffin?

Quayle   And him in it.

Jack, **Baggie**, **Quayle** *and* **Claxton** *leave.* **Einhildur** *comes over with a broom, sweeps.* **Snacker** *smiles at her.*

Snacker   Hi.

Einhildur   I am not chatting! Look at this mess!

Snacker   Einhildur?

Einhildur   So?

Snacker   I'm 'the snacker'.

Einhildur   *The* snacker?

Snacker   Like *the* bosun.

Einhildur   I'm *the* Einhildur. It means 'the lone warrior woman'.

Snacker   With lovely ears.

Einhildur   That's it! You are all checking out today.

She shoves the broom into **Snacker**'s *hands and huffs off behind the bar. The boys walk back in carrying a coffin.*

Einhildur   What is this now?!

Quayle   This is Harry Thorpe.

Jack   We'll need to fridge him. Cells'll be breaking down, farting.

Einhildur   I am not having a corpse in my hotel!

Claxton   Einhildur. It's just tonight. Ten minutes ago, remember, I paid for six men, six rooms.

Einhildur   You did not tell me one of them was dead.

Claxton   It's not even a night, we'll be leaving at five in the morning.

Einhildur *goes off in a huff.*

Jack   What's the plan? I ask, 'cause I'm having a finger taken off tomorrow.

Claxton   We're booked on the six o'clock flight to London.

Baggie   Flying? Nice.

Snacker   I don't want to fly.

Jack   Six o'clock?

Claxton   There's a taxi booked for four thirty.

Jack   We're not going to be sleeping then, fuck it. Get the beers in.

Quayle   Have you found any drink in this puritan hell hole?

Demonstrating how to make a drink.

Snacker   Pils, no alcohol, and Brennivin. Lot of alcohol.

Quayle (*drinking*)   Jaysus! That's terrible. I'd down a pint of cod liver oil over that any day.

Jack (*eating*)   Some of these chips are still warm.

Snacker   Any dreams lately, Michael?

Jack   Oh fuck, don't set him off.

Quayle   Last night's dream, I was sat in church, Catholic, I was naked, twas a wedding, and I'm trying to saw mi left leg off with a cake knife, and there's blood everywhere and I'm hacking away at myself above the knee and I'm wearing stockings, suspenders and a pair of snow skis but nothin' else and mi cock and balls are just hanging down for all to see, and the bride lifts her dress up and she's got no legs, just bicycle wheels and one of the tyres is flat and Morecambe and Wise are on their knees trying to find the puncture with a bowl of water and a bike pump, and I succeed in hacking mi leg off and I hop over to the bride and fit it into her hip and she hops out the church as happy as Larry. After that, I slept like a babby.

Jack   Don't eat cheese before bed.

Quayle   A dream is a storm. It washes away the previous day's pain, restores the balance of good and evil, and vomits up your clean, wet body onto the beach of life, ready for another day of pain and humiliation. Ain't that right, Mister Claxton?

Claxton   I guess. Did the doctors give you a death certificate for Harry?

Quayle   Aye.

He reaches into his coat and gives **Claxton** *an envelope.*

Claxton   What's it say?

Quayle   Says he's dead.

Claxton *glances at it, but doesn't read it.*

Jack   I'm sorry I punched you, Mister Claxton.

Claxton   That's alright.

Quayle   Did I miss something?

Baggie   Ha! We had a bar fight. It was like *Shane*, the western.

Jack   I'm sorry I got my cock out.

Claxton   That was entirely understandable.

Quayle   Now, I've seen the film *Shane* three times and I don't remember Alan Ladd ever getting his cock out.

Claxton   He's lost his favourite finger.

Jack   I fucking have, yeah.

Snacker   Donald? Do you play cards?

Claxton   I can.

Jack   That can't be right. A snacker calling the trawler owner 'Donald'.

Claxton   Snacker's a man. He's survived his ship going down.

Jack   How's that make him a man?

Claxton   In a kind of 'every man thinks meanly of himself for not having been a soldier, or not having been at sea'.

Baggie   Who said that?

Snacker   He did. Donald. Just then.

Claxton   Samuel Johnson.

Snacker   Michael Quayle here says there's only two sorts of men. In't that right, Michael?

Quayle   In what sense, Snacker?

Snacker   'The Ramsey Thing!'

Quayle   Aye.

Jack   Oh no not that load of bollocks!

Claxton   Tell me about the Ramsey Thing, Michael.

Quayle   I'm not sure you're man enough to handle the life-changing epiphany that is the unavoidable consequence of hearing the story.

Claxton   I'll not know until I've heard it.

Baggie   We've got till four in the morning.

Jack   That's not long enough.

Quayle   Be it on your own head, Mister Claxton. I ran away from me da at fourteen, and ended up a share fisherman out of Ramsey, Isle of Man –

Jack   – fourteen. Bollocks. It's made-up shit.

Quayle   We're tied up in Ramsey harbour. I'm on the deck mending nets and the Wicked Hen –

Snacker   – that's the skipper. Sorry, Michael. I love this story!

Quayle   The Wicked Hen is up on the quay gently manuring the minds of German tourists –

Snacker   – manuring! Ha, ha! Brilliant!

Quayle   – when he sort of whisper shouts down to me 'Michael, Michael, up here quick!' and I drop my needle and scramble up the ladder and he says, 'Look in the pram here, you'll never see the like of this.' And I see a little family, wife, husband and about five kids and the woman pushing one of them Silver Cross prams, and the Wicked Hen steps back with a nod and a 'lovely day for it!' to the party, and he lets them through, and I take a glance, as surrep-fucking-titious as you like, and I can't believe what I see, I stop breathing, and my face contorts ready to howl the terror out of me. In the pram is a living thing smiling at me, with a beard, three eyes, a hole for a mouth, and the face and head of a seventy-year-old man, but the body of a baby and wearing a nappy too, born of woman, the very woman there pushing it along, proud an'all, with a smile on her face. And the little family move off down the quay, and all I can hear is mi pulse banging in mi ears and the Wicked Hen leans in and says to me, 'There you go, Michael, you're a man now, and there's only two kinds of men, them who's seen the Ramsey Thing, and them that ain't.'

A window blows open, some glass is smashed.

Claxton   Jesus!

Quayle   You see, the gods are listening!

Jack   It's the wind!

Einhildur *runs over with a length of wood.*

Claxton   I went to see a ship once in Ramsey. I'd heard of the Ramsey Thing. I'm ashamed to say, I didn't believe a word of it.

Quayle   I seen it. You have not.

Snacker *is there to help* **Einhildur**.

Snacker   Hi.

Einhildur   Hold it shut will you.

She slots the wood across the shutters holding it closed, and then with a ratchet screwdriver screws the length into the shutter.

Thank you. The snacker.

Snacker   I'm here. For you. You know, to help.

Einhildur *retreats.*

Claxton   Michael, you were put off three days before the *Graham Greene* sank.

Quayle   I knew she was lost.

Claxton   How?

Jack   He'd had a whatsaname.

Snacker   A shit? A wank? A good breakfast?

Jack   No, a . . . when you can see the future.

Baggie   A premonition.

Enter **Einhildur** *with a dustpan and brush, some tape and some cardboard. During the next she tapes the cardboard to the glass hole, and sweeps the broken glass up.*

Jack (*nudging* **Snacker**)   Now's your chance, lad.

Snacker *goes over and helps her.*

Claxton   They say you're unlucky.

Quayle   The opposite.

He touches a small seal skin pouch around his neck.

I'm blessed, I was born with a veil.

Claxton   A caul?

Baggie   He never takes it off.

Jack   Gives him bad dreams.

Claxton   What would happen if you and your caul were separated?

Quayle   It would never. Served me well. I had a brother, Pascal, we was on a sidewinder out of Fleetwood. Off Cape Farewell, Greenland, we've hauled, and we're waiting on the mate to let the cod end out. Me and Pascal, we both had a little tab on the go. The mate pulls the rope, the bag opens up, and the cod tumble out. Pascal relights his tab, and takes down a long toke. The fish are tumbling into the pounds when out with them comes a Second World War German mine. It hits the deck and explodes, and a piece of shrapnel, like Myron's own fucking discus, flew through the air and sliced me brother's head clean off. I watched his smile, and his face, and his tab and his cap, fall into the fish washer, and the rest of him turned and walked towards me, no head, and with clear intent he put his arms around me, and I could feel the strength of his love, and I looked right down the hole in his neck into his lungs –

Jack   – it's all bollocks!

Quayle   – and I saw the smoke swirling around in his lungs, and I sees the black tobacco tar dripping off the white florets therein. And it was on that very day I gave up smoking.

Jack   Crap!

Baggie   How can his head fall into the fish washer when the fish washer is above his head?

Quayle   Pearls before swine, Donald. They don't want art, they want the prosaic bastard truth.

Claxton   But you were unscathed?

Quayle   I have no doubt Freud could write a fucking book about me alone.

Claxton   Last week, Friday, Stabba put a call through asking permission to put you off with internal bleeding.

Quayle   I faked it.

Claxton   Why?

Quayle   I'd seen Frank Calvert. Or his mist.

Jack   Ah, fuck it's endless. Baggie, d'yer hear that. Frank Calvert now!

Claxton   Who's Frank Calvert?

Baggie   Frank Calvert was a big old stoker, out of Hull, simple bloke, compliant. Worked the old coal burners before the war. Six foot six, and all muscle, even that bit between the ears.

Claxton   That's a pretty stupid size for a stoker, with all that bending.

Jack   Donald, it's all exaggeration.

Baggie   But he's seen sometimes.

Quayle   He's sent to mark the man that's wanted.

Jack   Jesus! Gimme strength.

Claxton   Wanted by whom?

Quayle   The big fellah. And he does that by leaving a black thumb print –

Baggie   – coal dust.

Quayle   It's ink.

Snacker   Must be coal dust, he's a stoker.

Jack   With a bad back.

Quayle   It's ink. Black thumb print on their foreheads.
There.

Claxton   You saw the ghost of Frank Calvert on the *Graham
Greene*?

Jack   This is why none of us like sailing with this bastard.

Quayle   I was on the winch –

Jack   – you're never on the fucking winch!

Quayle   – and there's no electric coming up so Stabba sent
me down to see that fellah there.

Points to the coffin.

Claxton   Harry Thorpe?

Quayle   I slip down the companionway towards the engine
room, and I'm thinking, 'It's unnatural quiet down here.'
And I notice the hatch to the engine room is closed, which
isn't normal – as a rule Harry would jam it open to get some
air in – but it's tight shut. My heart is bang bang banging
away and I know there is a power that is not human down
there –

Jack   – ooooohhh.

Quayle   – and I touch my caul, and I put my hand on the
hatch to open it and at that moment it flies open and I'm
thrown back against the wall and I can't see a man, but
there's a black mist, like a terrible malevolent power, which
has slipped past me and swept along the companionway. It's
gone, and suddenly I can hear the engines again, deafening.
And I start to fear what I might find when I go inside. I walk
round the steam generator, and there's Harry, the poor
fucker. Kneeling like he's at communion, and such a look of
terror on his face as I've never seen in my life before nor ever
want to again, and on his forehead is a black thumb print.

Claxton   But he's alive?

Quayle   Frozen, petrified and he looks at me and he can't speak, and I know Frank Calvert has chosen him and in choosing him he's chosen the *Graham Greene*, so I go back up to the pounds, I find meself a big daddy cod, cut the heart out of it, stick it in my mouth, I go up to the bridge, bite down on the heart and spit blood all over Stabba's precious charts. Stabba's not too displeased 'cause the nearest hospital is Helgafel, at the far end of the ground, and it'll give him a chance to take on fresh water.

Claxton   But Harry was alive –

Baggie   – he survived the sinking, I got him in the raft.

Claxton   Did he have a thumb print on his head?

Baggie   If he did, I didn't notice.

Jack   Quayle! You're a crap artist.

Quayle   I'm alive.

Claxton   So when did Harry die then?

Quayle   Last night, in the Reykjavik hospital. He died of fright.

Jack   Fright my arse! He'd been in the water.

Baggie   Exposure.

Quayle   You've got the death certificate there.

Claxton *looks at the document. Turns to a page he'd not read before.*

Claxton   Heart attack.

Quayle   Which ain't exposure.

Jack   You're a lying bastard, Quayle.

Quayle   Look on his forehead if you don't believe me.

Snacker   Open the coffin? Oh wow!

Quayle   And you'll see the mark of Frank Calvert.

Jack   I fucking will. It's only screws.

Baggie   No! I will not let this happen.

Jack   I want to see this thumb print!

*He goes to the window and finds **Einhildur**'s ratchet screwdriver.*

Claxton   But you saw the mark of Frank Calvert a full three days before the ship sank. He would've have washed it off.

Snacker   You've never have been to sea have you, Donald!

Jack *begins to unscrew the coffin screws.* **Einhildur** *appears.*

Einhildur   Hey! You can't just take the tools. What are you doing? This is a hotel not a morgue.

Baggie   No! Jack! I'll not let you. Stop it.

*He drags **Jack** away from the coffin with the screwdriver. The screwdriver is dropped as **Jack** and **Baggie** struggle with each other. **Snacker** takes over unscrewing the screws.*

Jack   Piss off, Baggie. I'm gonna prove Quayle a liar!

Baggie   He's a dead man. Leave him in peace.

Jack   Peace?! I have to listen to Quayle's crap day in and day out!

*As they struggle **Snacker** continues with the unscrewing.*

Einhildur   Leave him in the box please!

Quayle *blocks* **Einhildur**.

Einhildur   Mister Claxton. You're in charge of your men, aren't you?!

Claxton   Snacker, just do the lid. I can't see any harm in this.

Einhildur   Why are you opening the coffin?!

Claxton   We want to see if Harry has a thumb print on his forehead.

Snacker   Put there by the ghost of Frank Calvert.

Einhildur   A ghost?!

Claxton   It's important, please miss.

Snacker *does the final screw. He lifts the lid and puts it to one side. They tentatively gather around, stooping down and looking at Harry's forehead.*

Quayle   There. Can you see it?

Jack   'kin'ell!

Claxton   Good Lord!

Snacker *faints and is caught by* **Einhildur**.

Einhildur   The snacker! He's fainted.

Claxton *and* **Einhildur** *attend to* **Snacker**. **Baggie** *faces off with* **Quayle**.

Baggie   Why did you do this?

Quayle   It's what I do.

Baggie   Did you not give a thought for Harry's dignity?

Quayle   Dignity? Three weeks sharing a fo'c's'le the size of a prison cell with eight other fools, sucking in their farts, their ciggy smoke, pissing on yer hands five times a day to convince the blood of life that it's still worth the flow. The day he went fishing was the day he lost his dignity.

Jack   He's admitting it! Quayle put the ink stain on Harry. Ha! He's a fucking head case.

Snacker *comes round and sees that his head is being supported in* **Einhildur**'*s lap.*

Snacker   Hi.

Einhildur   Hi.

Claxton   You fainted.

Snacker   Did I?

Einhildur   Yes.

Snacker   Did you catch me?

Einhildur   Only just.

Snacker   Are you going to look after me?

Einhildur   No. I've done enough.

She lets **Snacker***'s head drop to the boards, with a bit of a thud.*

Snacker   Argh!

Einhildur   This coffin cannot stay here. What kind of place has a coffin in the foyer?

Jack   A mortuary, an undertaker's.

Einhildur   Don't get funny with me, I'm not laughing!

Snacker   A coffin museum.

Einhildur (*beat*)   That is funny. I will give you the key to room 6 and you will carry him in there, out of sight, now!

She gives the keys to **Jack***.* **Baggie** *is washing the stain off of Harry's head.*

Claxton (*to* **Quayle**)   But if you made all this up, there goes your reason for getting put off.

Quayle   At last! An intellect to match mi own! It's February, off Iceland, no sane man would go fishing. Am I wrong?

Baggie   Every man on that ship knew the weather was turning. But no one else asked to be put off.

Quayle   They're all Hull men and have a bond of affiliation stronger than chains. You can't be seen to want to leave a ship, and if you ever did, your cowardice would be the only talk in Rayners. And years after you've gone to meet your maker, folks would be tarring your sons with the same yellow brush.

Jack   You're the coward.

Quayle   As if wanting to stay alive is a failure of manhood. You've always been antipathetic to my cause Jack.

Jack   Don't you fucking call me pathetic!

Quayle   Yer don't even understand yer own language.

Claxton   You're not a Hull man, so you're free?

Quayle   I'm half mad, half Irish, half Manx and a hundred per cent immune to fucking gossip, yes.

Baggie *sings by the coffin.*

Baggie
  Ooooooooooold faithful, we'll roam the range together

Snacker (*singing*)
  When the red, red robin –

Jack   – shut it, Snacker! They was both Hull FC fans.

Snacker   Yeah, and I'm Rovers.

Jack   He's saying goodbye to his best man.

Baggie
  Ooooooooooold faithful, in any kind of weather

Snacker (*singing*)
  When the red, red robin comes bob, bob, bobbin' along –

Baggie/Jack
  – shoot the bastard, shoot the bastard!

Baggie
  When the round-up days are over
  And the Boulevard's white with clover,
  For you Old Faithful pal of mine.

A silence. **Baggie** *replaces the lid of the coffin.*

Einhildur   Come on!

Jack (*to* **Claxton**)   Giss hand then. You killed him.

Claxton, Jack, Baggie *and* **Quayle** *lift the coffin off.*

Einhildur   Through here.

Left alone, **Snacker** *takes his chance and sidles up to* **Einhildur.**

Snacker   Hi.

Einhildur   What?

Snacker   Is this your hotel then?

Einhildur   Yes.

Snacker   Wow! Impressive. I mean, you're only, er . . .

Einhildur   – I'm only what?

Snacker   A girl.

Einhildur   What?!

Snacker   I meant, young. You're only young.

Einhildur   My grandpa bought it, then died. Then my grandmother died. Then my mother –

Snacker   – she died?! Oh no.

Einhildur   She ran off to Miami with an American airman.

Snacker   Thank God for that. So it's yours now?

Einhildur   It is in my mother's name but we are not talking and I can't make any decisions and I do all the work. Is that enough?

Snacker   So it's kinda yours but it isn't. Which is why you're grumpy.

Einhildur   What is grumpy?

Snacker   Grumpy suits you. Can I do my card trick, around the room?

Einhildur   I don't care anymore.

Snacker *rejoins the table.*

Snacker   I'm gonna do my trick.

Claxton   Are you a magician?

Snacker   Not really, Donald.

Claxton   What's the trick, Snacker?

Snacker   I bought a book didn't I.

Jack   I didn't know you could read.

Snacker   *You Too Can Have a Superpower Memory.* I've trained mi mind an't I. Someone needs to distribute these cards around the room here, and I memorise them, all fifty, er . . . how many cards in a pack? I've forgotten.

Jack   You've forgotten?

Baggie   Superpower memory.

Jack   Fifty-two.

Claxton   I'll do that.

Snacker *hands the cards over.*

Claxton   Anywhere?

Snacker   Put them all over the room. One by one.

Claxton *puts one on a shelf.*

Claxton   Here?

Snacker   Yeah, yeah. Anywhere.

Einhildur *turns the TV on. It is a small, wall-mounted TV that feels as if it is more for the staff than customers.* **Claxton** *starts distributing the cards. One on a shelf, one on another table, one on the bar.* **Einhildur** *notices this.*

Einhildur   The snacker? What is this now?

Snacker   I said, my card trick. I've trained mi brain an't I.

Einhildur   That is so obvious.

Snacker   My friend Donald is gonna place the cards all over the lobby, and I will memorise all –

Jack   – fifty-two!

Einhildur   Mister Claxton is your friend?

Snacker   He's the trawler owner.

Einhildur   He is the capitalist? And you are the worker.

Snacker   Yeah, rich man.

Einhildur   He has money for chips.

Snacker   He has a farm, a big farm like, with a cleaner and that.

Einhildur   He has a cleaner?

Snacker   She cleans the house, not the farm, that'd be silly, 'cause the farm don't need cleaning being mainly fields and that. He's like, I mean look at him, he's proper, brogue shoes, and clothes from like a shop, not the market. You wimme?

Einhildur   I am wimme, yes. He is a quality human being. So what does that make you? What is the opposite of quality?

Snacker   I'm nowt. I'm a deckie learner.

Einhildur   With stupid clothes.

Snacker   We was given these, I din't choose these did I. I look like a fucking Mexican.

Einhildur   Next time you might die.

Snacker   There won't be a next time. That's my last trip.

Einhildur   Last trip for all of you. The Athling vote tonight.

Snacker   The what?

Einhildur *indicates the television above the bar.*

Einhildur   This. Our Parliament. We're going for two hundred.

Snacker   Two hundred what?

Einhildur   Miles! Fishing waters.

Snacker   What do you want? Another cod war?

Einhildur   Yes! We're very bad like that. We always win, so why not?

Snacker *stares at the TV, intrigued.* **Einhildur** *looks at her watch and takes menus over to the table.*

Jack   Our snacker, he likes you, luv.

Einhildur   I know. I am not stupid. Would you boys like some wine?

Jack   Wine?!

Baggie   I thought you was teetotal here.

Jack   That's why we're drinking this shit.

Einhildur   If you buy food, I become a restaurant, and in Iceland you can buy Spanish wine. Only Spanish.

Claxton   No French wine?

Einhildur   Of course not. Iceland does not sell cod to France.

Quayle   I'm starving. I could eat the holy lamb out of God's right hand and fuck the consequences.

Einhildur   I have Rioja blanco, Rioja red or Vinho Verde.

Jack   What colour's Vinho Verde?

Claxton   White. What are we eating?

Einhildur   Fish.

Claxton   Of course. Then a bottle of the white Rioja I think.

Jack   A bottle each.

Einhildur   Five bottles of white Rioja?

Claxton   Absolutely, we're not sleeping, we're staying up.

Snacker   Never had wine. What's it like?

Jack   Makes me argumentative.

Baggie   Don't take much to set you off anyhow.

Jack   Fuck off!

Claxton   So how do you rememeber fifty-two cards,
Snacker? Presumably mnemonics?

Snacker   No, it's a kind of memory aid system.

Claxton *picks up a card from a round table. The queen of hearts.*

Snacker   For each card you mek up a mental painting –

Claxton   – a painting?

Snacker   For this one, the queen of hearts, it's on this round
table, so I'm gonna imagine I'm having sex with the Queen
on a roundabout.

Jack   A roundabout?!

Snacker   Yeah, like Scotch Corner on the A1.

Claxton   Because it's a round table?

Baggie   How do you know it's not the queen of spades or –

Snacker   – so in mi mental picture the Queen's cut her
heart out, and is tryna give it to me while we're on the job.

Claxton   Complicated.

He points out a card under the flower vase on a different table.

This one under the flowers.

Snacker   What is it?

Claxton   Two of clubs.

Snacker *closes his eyes painting a mental picture.*

Snacker   I'm shagging a shoe in a flower bed.

Claxton   Shoe – two?

Snacker   You got it.

Jack   Eh, Baggie, he's fucking a shoe now.

Claxton   Clubs?

Snacker   And Fred Flintstone is hitting me on the arse with a big wooden club.

Claxton *moves on.*

Claxton   This one under the tankard. Five of diamonds.

Snacker *closes his eyes and concentrates.*

Jack   Who are you fucking this time, Snack?

Snacker   A bee hive.

They laugh.

Baggie   A beehive?

Claxton   Hive. Five. Diamonds?

Snacker   The beehive is shaped like a diamond.

Jack (*laughing*)   I've never fucked a beehive, is it worth the aggravation?

Claxton *is by the phone.*

Claxton   This one. Jack of clubs.

Snacker   I'm picturing a young man, on the phone, wearing a tie, that gives you the club, jack of clubs.

Claxton   How does a tie give you clubs?

Jack   Clubs is Fred Flintstone innit?

Snacker   Anything in your pictures wearing a tie, like a golf club tie, is a club. A tree wearing a tie?

Claxton   Tree of clubs. Three of clubs.

Snacker   So a young bloke, wearing a tie, making a phone call is jack of clubs.

Jack   Are you bumming him when he's talking on the phone?

Snacker   No.

Jack   Why not?

Snacker   'Cause I like girls.

Quayle   Ha, ha, Snacker, he's a phenomenon.

Einhildur *comes out with five bottles of white Rioja. She puts them on the table, unopened.*

Einhildur   Five bottles of white Rioja.

Claxton   Thank you.

Einhildur   I'll get a corkscrew.

Claxton   No need.

Claxton *whips out a Swiss Army knife, and unfurls the corkscrew.*

Quayle   A Swiss Army knife, eh?

Claxton   Thankfully, the Swiss believe that modern warfare is mainly drinking fine wine, eating cheese, filing your nails, screwing and origami.

Quayle   Origami?

Claxton   The scissors.

Quayle   That's quite a routine that one. Does it ever get a laugh?

Claxton   Sometimes.

Quayle   Shame there isn't a tool on there to winkle you out of spending the night with us four drunken cunts.

Claxton   To be honest, Michael, I'd rather be here than Hull. At the moment.

Jack   You've done your walk though?

Claxton   Two days ago.

Jack   That'll have given you a story.

Quayle   They say man is unique 'cause of these oppositional thumbs God give us, but for me it's the chat.

Claxton   Story telling?

Quayle   If we do a brave and noble thing, the only reason is so we can craft a story, and thereby become immortal.

Snacker   Entertainment innit.

Quayle   Deeper than that, young fellah. It's a way of declaring yourself to the world.

Claxton *pops a cork.*

Quayle   Baggie! Tell Donald about the day your da was slain by this industry.

Claxton   Your father was a trawlerman?

Jack   We're West Hull, worr else is there?

Baggie   My father was on the *Endon.*

Silence. **Baggie** *is affected. Chokes.*

Jack   D'yer see that? Grown man, crying.

Baggie   H161 out of Hull. 1933.

Jack   Never been explained. No compensation, no money.

Claxton   I'd like Baggie to tell me. If that's alright. Jack?

Jack   Fuck's sake.

Einhildur   You're not buying fish, you're buying men's lives.

Jack   We say that in Hull an'all.

Einhildur   So, now you know that Hull does not have a monopoly on poetry.

Baggie   The *Endon* was one of the old Red Cross Boxing fleet. It was a Christmas trip and on the way out the mate was lost overboard in the Humber so she returned to Hull –

Jack   – unlucky.

Claxton   To lose the mate?

Jack   To break a trip, and return to port. Dick.

Quayle   Hey.

Baggie   They take on a new mate. Albert Bagnal.

Claxton   Your father.

Jack   Broken trip now innit!

Baggie   Next time the Endon is seen is Christmas Eve, by the *St Kilda*. The weather's fine and the skipper of the *St Kilda* pulls alongside hoping to share a Christmas dram with the Endon's skipper. And then they sense summat inexplicable.

Snacker (*spooky noise*)   Whoooooooooooo!

Baggie   The Endon had all her lights on but there's not a soul on deck and no skipper on the bridge. The bosun of the *St Kilda* goes aboard with a couple of lads, and shouts back that there's no one below neither, no one under the whaleback, and no one in the engine room.

Claxton   Any fish in the fish room?

Jack (*kicks his chair back and stands*)   Ha! There yer go! All the owner's interested in is money! Is there any fish in the fish room! He's talking about his father.

Quayle   It's a relevant question. If there's fish in the fish room, we know they've been fishing. So sit your stupid arse back down eejit.

Baggie   The fish room's full of fish, it's good weather, she's not taking water, nowt wrong with it.

Claxton   Engines?

Baggie   Coal burner. The fire was out. No steam.

Claxton   Lifeboats?

Baggie   Untouched.

Jack   Have a drink, Baggie.

Baggie *drinks the wine.*

Baggie   They put a cable on to tow her and the bosun stays on the *Endon* in the wheelhouse, but as soon as they start to pull a breeze comes up, not much at first, but out of nothing there's a swell and in five minutes there's a helluva blow on, howling round the two ships tied together and it's making the whole operation dangerous, and the bosun is waving his shirt out the wheelhouse window as if to say –

Jack   – get me the fuck off o' this!

Baggie   And they cut the line to the *Endon* and just as they're wondering how to save the bosun, he leaps over the gunwale with a high jump and he's in the swell. They chuck him a belt and haul him out the water, and just as sudden as it come the weather fines away, instantly, the wind, the swell, fines away, and all is returned to this lifeless, deadly calm, and silence.

Claxton   Extraordinary.

Jack   He an't finished. Tell him about the snacker.

Baggie   A week later another trawler hauled its nets and inside they found the body of a young lad –

Jack   – the *Endon*'s snacker –

Snacker   – oh no, that's me!

Baggie   – with such a mask of horror on the kid's face they chose not to bring him home to his mother, so they threw him back over the wall.

Quayle   There can be no disputing there's a power out there.

Claxton   God?

Baggie   Fate.

Jack   That's all there is. If it's got your name on it, that's it.

Quayle (*sings*)
I thought I heard the Old Man say
'Leave her, Johnny, leave her'
Tomorrow ye will get your pay
And it's time for us to leave her

Jack   Fucking hate sea shanties.

Snacker *joins in with a stomping a beat:*

Leave her, Johnny, leave her
Oh, leave her, Johnny, leave her
For the voyage is long and the winds don't blow
And it's time for us to leave her

Jack   Elvis! Roy Orbison.

I hate to sail on this stinking old tub
Leave her, Johnny, leave her
No grog allowed and rotten grub
And it's time for us to leave her

Jack   Dion. 'Runaround Sue'.

Leave her, Johnny, leave her
Oh, leave her, Johnny, leave her
For the voyage is long and the winds don't blow
And it's time for us to leave her

Einhildur *brings a whalemeat starter.*

Baggie   Here we go!

Claxton   Looks great. What is it?

Einhildur   This is whale.

Claxton   Whale meat?

Einhildur   Of course.

Snacker (*singing*)
 Whale meat again!
 Don't know where,
 Don't know when,
 But I know whale meat again.
 Some sunny day.

Claxton   Smashing. Thank you.

Snacker (*speaking to* **Einhildur**)   Do you like David Bowie?

Einhildur   I do, yes.

Snacker   The Spiders are from Hull.

Einhildur   David Bowie is from Hull?

Snacker   No. The Spiders. David Bowie's band, they're all from Hull.

Einhildur   I thought they were from Mars.

Snacker   Mars? Why would they come from Mars. No one lives on Mars.

Einhildur (*beat*)   The Spiders from Mars.

Snacker   Oh yeah. You're right. One nil.

Quayle   You're lucky to get nil, Snacker.

Snacker   Bowie's bassist, Trev Bolder, I went to school with his brother, Andy.

Einhildur   Impressive.

Snacker   Yeah. He used to nick mi milk.

Einhildur   I like Captain Beefheart.

Snacker   OK.

Einhildur   And the Grateful Dead.

Snacker   Alright. Gary Glitter?

Einhildur   No. The snacker, I am busy.

Claxton *is eating the whale-meat starter.*

Claxton   Coo! Strong flavours.

Einhildur   That's shark.

Quayle   Left to rot in the sand, marinating in human urine.

Claxton   I'm definitely getting the urine.

Baggie   This is the whale. It's good. Like tuna.

Claxton   Christ! Give me some of that Rioja.

Quayle   Einhildur! Do you have a fishing story? A young buck Romeo taken from you by the rapacious capitalist's lust for cod.

Einhildur   I have no connections with fishing.

Quayle   Any kind of verbal pageant would do for us.

Einhildur   We have a ghost story in Iceland.

Quayle   We're not gonna bed, we're killing time. The floor is yours, darlin'.

Einhildur *tells her story from behind the bar.* **Snacker** *joins in playing characters.*

Einhildur   There was a priest, living in Djákninn á Myrká. You would translate that as Dark Water. And the priest loved Gudrun.

Snacker   What's Gudrun?

Einhildur   It's a girl's name.

Snacker   Oh, I thought it was like Marmite. The priest loved Marmite. The priest loved Gudrun.

Jack   Funny kind of priest, in love with a girl.

Einhildur   Lutheran. Not Catholic. Our priests are always falling in love. Vicar maybe.

Snacker   I'll be the vicar.

He plays the vicar to **Einhildur**'s *Gudrun.*

Einhildur   The vicar had a horse called Faxi, and he used to ride the horse, a long way, to see Gudrun.

Jack (*to* **Snacker**)   That's like you getting two buses to Bilton Grange to see your Janice.

Snacker *grabs a broom to be the horse.* **Snacker** *and* **Einhildur** *mime out the story.* **Einhildur** *finds that she enjoys it.*

Einhildur   The week before Christmas the vicar rode out to see Gudrun, crossing the two rivers on the ice bridges.

Snacker *canters around the bar on the broom.* **Einhildur** *waits for him, sees the value.*

Jack   The fuck you doing, Snack?!

Snacker   I'm the vicar.

Einhildur   Gudrun's mother cooked a dinner, and the vicar asked for her permission to marry Gudrun, which she gave. When he left he promised he would return on Christmas Eve and take her to Dark Water for the Christmas festival at the end of which they would marry. He set off home in high spirits on his horse Faxi –

Jack   – yer've set off again, Snack.

Snacker *sets off again.*

Einhildur   – but when he got to the river he was unable to cross as there had been a sudden thawing and the ice bridge had been swept away. He found a second ice bridge but when he was halfway across it collapsed and he was plunged into the torrent of the river.

Snacker   Don't drink and drive.

Einhildur   The next morning a farmer found the horse dead, and further along the vicar too, on a sand bank. The farmer rode to Dark Water with the body and the villagers buried their vicar in his own churchyard.

Jack   Did they tell Gudrun?

Einhildur   They couldn't get to her because the ice bridges had collapsed.

Snacker   Why didn't they phone her?

Einhildur   This is 1760.

Snacker   So?

Baggie   Telephones were invented in eighteen summat.

Snacker   Oh fuck.

Einhildur   So Gudrun was never told her fiancé was dead. On Christmas Eve she is dressed and waiting for the vicar to come and take her to Dark Water for their wedding. There is a knock at the door and Gudrun's mother opens it, but there is no one there.

Snacker   Wooooooo. Spooky.

Einhildur   Gudrun grabs her coat, and walks out into the night. She sees the vicar standing by his horse.

Jack   The vicar! The horse! Snacker! Come on!

Snacker   I thought he was dead.

Baggie   His ghost.

Snacker *plays the vicar/horse.*

Einhildur   Gudrun sees the vicar standing by his horse.

Snacker *picks up the broom.*

Einhildur   They kiss.

Quayle   They kiss.

Snacker *and* **Einhildur** *make a move to kiss but don't kiss.*

Einhildur   The vicar lifts her on to the horse. He gets on the horse in front of her and they ride to Dark Water. When they get to the village the vicar rides the horse straight into the graveyard and stops before an open grave.

She opens the trap to the beer cellar.

The vicar dismounts and says to Gudrun 'come with me, Garoon, come with me' and he steps into the grave.

Snacker *steps down the cellar steps.*

Snacker   Come with me, Garoon!

Einhildur   'You waited for me, Garoon, come with me.'

Snacker   You waited for me, Garooon, come with me.

Einhildur   And Gudrun realises that this is a ghost and that her lover must be dead, and she turns to run, but the ghost grabs her and pulls at her coat, dragging her into the grave. And the soil begins to fill the grave and she is getting buried with him, but she slides out of her coat and crawls from the grave just in time to see the vicar drowning in the mud and screaming, 'Garoon, come to me, I love you!'

Snacker   Garoon! Come to me, I love you!

Einhildur   And finally he disappears under the piles of earth and is buried.

Snacker *shuts the trap door on himself.* **Claxton**, **Quayle** *and* **Baggie** *applaud.*

Jack   Bloody hell.

Einhildur   The next day the villagers drag a huge stone and set it over the grave so that the vicar could never leave and torment Gudrun again.

Jack *stands on the trap so* **Snacker** *can't get out. He's laughing.* **Snacker** *is banging.*

Quayle   Let the lad out of there!

Snacker *opens the trap.*

Snacker   Why did he call her Garoon when her name was Gudrun?

Einhildur   Ghosts in Iceland, can't say God, and Gudrun means God's Rune.

Snacker   Oooooo. Garoon, come to me, I love you!

Claxton   Does that grave exist?

Einhildur   Of course. What am I? A bullshit artist?!

Snacker   My uncle saw a ghost once in Hull, on Spring Bank West. In the sidecar of a motorbike and sidecar.

Jack   Fuck.

Snacker   Yeah.

Baggie   How did your dad know it was a ghost?

Snacker   I dunno.

Jack   Was he holding his head or summat?

Snacker   No.

Claxton   Was this daytime?

Snacker   Yeah.

Claxton   Had your uncle been drinking?

Snacker   No, he was driving his van.

Silence.

Jack   Is that it?

Snacker   Yeah.

Quayle   Snacker, if I were you, I'd hang on to that story, 'cause the film rights must be worth a fucking fortune.

Einhildur *smashes a plate behind the bar.*

Jack   Snacker! Go on.

Snacker   Garoon, come to me, I love you!

He stands and goes over.

Einhildur   It was an accident.

Snacker   Let me do that, you're cooking. Have you got a dustpan and brush?

Einhildur   Under there.

Snacker *goes behind the bar and starts sweeping up the mess.*

Snacker   Ring your mother.

Einhildur   What?

Snacker   Talk to your mother. If she says she's staying in Miami, you'll know where you are. She might give you the hotel. Gotta talk. Can't go on like this can you.

Einhildur   No. No. I don't believe it can be done, the cards. All fifty-two.

Snacker   I've done it before.

He finishes sweeping and goes back to learning the cards. **Jack** *stands and goes behind the bar, with a wink to* **Baggie** *and* **Quayle***.*

Baggie   When you did the walk –

Quayle   – the fucking walk? Jaysus if I'd have died would they make you walk all the way to the Isle of Man?

Claxton   That's how it works, you walk to every widow's house.

Quayle   What about the walk to the magistrates' court in chains for jumping ship. Deckhands, chained to each other, walked through the open streets like African slaves. Fifty years after Wilberforce and in his own fucking town an'all.

Snacker   City.

Claxton   How did you vote, Michael? Stay in the EEC or leave?

Quayle   I wouldn't vote for the free movement of capital and labour, and the further exploitation of the working man.

Claxton   Leave then?

Quayle   I'm Irish, I didn't get a fucking vote.

Jack *appears from behind the bar with a knife, unseen by* **Claxton**, *but showing it to* **Quayle**. *He sits back down, the knife now secreted.*

Baggie   I was asking, on the walk, did you go to Stabba's? Sproatley innit? Did you go out that far?

Claxton   I didn't actually speak to Mrs Stabba.

Baggie   Ha!

Jack   What are you laughing at?

Baggie   'Mrs Stabba'.

Claxton   Actually –

Jack   – actually.

Claxton   Why did they call Jim 'Stabbasausage'?

Baggie   You never heard him say Stabbasausage?

Claxton   Never.

Baggie   He didn't like to swear, so if he was annoyed instead of swearing he'd say 'Stabbasausage'.

Jack   He'd swear if he lost a net.

Claxton   What would he say when he lost a net?

Jack   Stabbafuckingsausage.

Baggie   I never heard him swear.

Jack   Never heard him swear?! I'll not let you get away with this, Baggie, just cos he's dead. He swore all the time. Stabbafuckingsausage or FuckmeStabbafuckingsausage!

Baggie   He's dead! I don't like that we talk ill –

Jack   – Baggie?! His own wife called him Stabbafuckingsausage!

Quayle   You didn't see her then on your pilgrimage?

Claxton   Who?

Jack   Mrs Stabbafuckingsausage!

Claxton   I didn't speak to her, no.

Quayle   Could've topped herself. Dead on the bathroom floor.

Jack   Na!

Quayle   The men die and the women are left with nothing but the eternal glory of their widowhood.

Einhildur   The cod will be ten minutes yet.

Quayle   Are you joining us, girl?

Einhildur   I'm making sure the Snacker's not cheating.

Quayle   He's an honest man is our Snacker, I've shipped with him twice now. I kind of love him.

Jack   Ha!

Snacker   You love me, Michael?

Quayle   I love your difference. You're not a fisherman. All of us here, we've got something in the blood that calls us to hunt the last wild food.

Snacker   I have a theory about that, about who I am.

Jack   He's got a 'theory' 'bout why he's such a useless twat!

Claxton   We're all listening!

Snacker *stops learning the cards, comes over and sits next to* **Einhildur** *at the table.*

Snacker   I don't have it in the blood, fishing.

Jack   Your dad's been fishing all his life!

Quayle   Let the man talk!

Snacker   One day Dill and Lighthouse are down Hessle Road –

Einhildur   – Dill and Lighthouse?

Jack   Dillinger.

Baggie   Walter Denton.

Claxton   Known for riding horses into pubs.

Jack   And sticking fireworks up his arse.

Baggie   Lighthouse is his mate. Massive tall bloke, with only one eye.

Snacker   And a white T shirt with red hoops. Lighthouse?

He winks slowly, repeatedly.

Get it?

Einhildur   Yes. Ha!

Snacker   So they're on Hessle Road outside Boyses –

Claxton   – a multi-faceted retail outlet.

Snacker   And there's about fifteen prams all with babies in.

Claxton   This is in the days when mums could leave their babies outside a shop.

Jack   I know this one. You're too young to remember this, Snack!

Snacker   There's them big fancy prams –

Baggie – Silver Cross.

Snacker – yeah, crappy buggies, all sorts. Fifteen of them.

Jack Ten when I fost heard it.

Snacker Dillinger swaps all the babies around. Every single baby gets picked up and put in a different pram.

Einhildur No, no, no?!

Baggie Famous story this.

Einhildur Oh my God!

Snacker So every baby, every baby, is in the wrong pram.

Einhildur Horrible!

Snacker And then all the mams come out.

Baggie Ha! Like world war three!

Snacker Screaming, crying, collapsing on the street. And Dillinger and Lighthouse are sat on the wall pissing themselves.

Einhildur Oh, this is so crazy!

Baggie That's Dillinger for you.

Quayle How does this explain your wonderful, preternatural fucking uselessness?

Snacker I was one of them babies.

Einhildur No?!

Jack Ha ha ha!

Snacker I never went back in the right pram. That is why I have no fishing blood. Probably mi father's a dentist or a school teacher or summat.

Einhildur Oh, the Snacker. That is horrible! And the wrong mother too!

Snacker Yeah.

Baggie   Dillinger. Madman.

Claxton   There is of course a Marxist analysis of the role and function of Dillinger.

Jack   Of course there fucking is. A what?

Claxton   Dillinger was functional to the industry. A colourful, charismatic entertainer, and the subject of many stories, and a mythology built up around him. He became an icon and every boy growing up on Hessle Road that had to suffer sharing a bedroom with two sisters couldn't wait to get away, to go to sea, to go fishing, to be like Dillinger, even though this is the most dangerous industry there is. If he hadn't existed, we, the owners, would've invented him.

Jack   Your end of the industry in't that dangerous is it?

The phone rings. **Einhildur** *leaps up to get it.*

Einhildur   Oh the Snacker, that is a really horrible story!

She goes to the bar. She checks in with the Althing on the TV.

Jack   You're in there, Snack. She called you by your fost name.

Claxton   Do you look like your father?

Snacker   Nope.

Claxton   Your mother?

Snacker   I hope not.

Claxton   Very unlikely.

Baggie   His dad is competent, a good trawlerman.

Jack   But our Snacker's fucking useless.

Claxton   There's more to life than fishing.

Snacker   I have a superpower memory.

Einhildur   Mister Baggie. Your wife!

Jack   Here you go. I bet she's had it.

Baggie *gets up and goes to the phone.*

Claxton   You ready? For the cards?

Snacker   Yeah. I've done that half of the room.

*They listen to **Baggie** on the phone aping his 'Ayes'.*

Baggie (*on the phone*)   It's me . . . aye . . . aye . . . aye . . . aye alright . . . aye . . . she shouldn't be allowed to go to bingo . . . it's not the first time she's been banned for fighting is it? . . . Alright I'm sorry . . . aye . . . aye . . . aye . . . aye . . . love you, tarra.

He puts the phone down.

Claxton   Have you ever married, Michael?

Quayle   I wouldn't be able to make the commitment. I walked out of *Gone with the Wind* and that's only four hours.

Claxton   Ha! Come on then, Snacker.

Claxton *and* **Snacker** *stand. During the following they go around the room with* **Claxton** *picking the card up. Looking at it, and* **Snacker** *saying the card.*

Claxton   This one.

Snacker   Four of spades.

Claxton   Well done!

Snacker   Put it back, 'cause I want to impress Einhildur, later.

Baggie *rejoins the table.*

Jack   She had it yet?

Baggie   No, she rang 'cause she won at bingo.

Jack   How much?

Baggie   Half a pound of lamb's liver.

Jack   I thought she were in hospital?

Baggie   She's having it at home.

Jack *shows* **Quayle** *the knife.*

Quayle   What's that gonna do for yers, Jack?

Jack (*quietly*)   Shhh! It's for him.

Snacker   Seven of spades.

Claxton   Correct!

Quayle   You're gonna murder the poor fool are ye?

Jack   We're gonna do it. The three of us. A pact. But Baggie dun't want in, even with Harry dead.

Baggie   Put it away.

Jack   See. You and me then, Michael.

Quayle   You and I.

Jack   You're in then?

Quayle   No. I was correcting your grammar.

Snacker   Er . . . King of hearts.

Claxton   Brilliant!

Jack   Fizz is dead. Why is that cunt still living when my best china is dead?

He hides the knife as **Einhildur** *delivers plates and cutlery.*

Snacker   Ace of diamonds.

Claxton   Yes!

Einhildur *retreats.*

Einhildur   Is it working?

Claxton   He's getting them!

Snacker   Ring your mother.

Einhildur *thinks for a beat, then goes behind the bar and dials.*
Snacker *looks over the bar at her and mimes 'she's on the phone' to*
Claxton.

Snacker   Her mother, in America.

Jack   Trawler owner, that's the only job in this industry
where there's no chance of dying. Well there is now.

He sticks the knife in the table.

Quayle   You're grieving. You should be dead. Right now,
you're not normal.

Snacker   Jack of spades!

Claxton   Correct!

Jack *stands violently, pulls the knife out of the table and conceals*
it.

Jack (*to* **Claxton**)   I've gorra story! A true story. An 'orror
story.

Claxton   For me?

Jack   Aimed at you, yeah.

Claxton   You've done well there, so far, Snacker. I'll sit
down.

Jack   Fill your glass.

Claxton *fills everyones glasses.* **Snacker** *goes over to* **Einhildur**.

Snacker   You alright, love?

Einhildur *shows her face. She's been crying.*

Einhildur   Who is Janice?

Snacker   Bilton Grange Janice?

Einhildur   Is she your girlfriend?

Snacker   Last year, yeah. It's all over with her. She's gone all
skinhead.

Einhildur   Skinhead?

Snacker   Had a budgie cut. She's now a festival of Fred Perry sportswear.

Jack   Oi! My story! Sit yersens over here!

Snacker   What's your mam say?

Einhildur   She's staying in Miami. She married him.

Snacker   Yeah?

Einhildur   She's giving me the hotel.

Snacker   Yeah!

Claxton   Einhildur! Story time!

Einhildur *hugs* **Snacker**. *The others watch, slightly amazed.*

Jack   Woah!

Quayle   Take your time, lad.

Baggie   Did I miss summat?

Einhildur *and* **Snacker** *join the group.*

Snacker   What?

Claxton   Jack's story.

Jack *stands.*

Jack   Right! You, you don't own me no more. Right?

Claxton   I never did.

Jack   The day my ship went down, three days ago, on that day, you stopped my money.

Claxton   That is how it is, yes.

Jack   Casual labour. This is a story about casual labour. My best mate at school, Tommy Hoodless –

Snacker   – Hoodless? As in what, he didn't have a hood?

Jack   Hoodless was his name.

Snacker   Why was it his name? Did he have a duffle coat with no hood?

Jack   It was his fucking dad's name.

Snacker   I thought it was a nickname. Sorry.

Jack   Tommy was my best mate at Trinity school. One winter he signed on the *Roderigo*.

Baggie   Oh no.

Jack   Yeah, it's that story. The *Roderigo* –

Claxton   – 800 tons.

Jack   You what?

Quayle   Leave it, Jack.

Jack   This is my story. If I want to tell 'em it was 800 tons I fucking will.

Claxton   I apologise.

Jack   The *Roderigo* was a big sidewinder, 800 tons, 1955 she went fishing off Iceland in January, and they're on the fish, and alongside is another Hull ship, the *Lorella*. The two skippers are big mates and they chat going up and down the ground on the VHF. Then it blows up, an east-southeasterly, difficult conditions, freezing hard, and on both ships the cables and the upperworks ice up.

Einhildur   The centre of gravity rises, very dangerous.

Quayle   Well done.

Einhildur   I'm Icelandic.

Jack   The two ships agree to clew the gear and run for shelter in Ritur Huk, but another Hull trawler comes through on the VHF, the *Kingston Garnet*, she's snagged her prop, no power, helpless, just sat out there in a force 10, icing up, can't even dodge.

Einhildur   Oh no.

Jack (*to* **Claxton**)   So, what do these *casual* labourers do? Eh?

Claxton   You turn around, and go back out into the storm to help them.

Jack   The *Kingston Garnet*'s helpless in the storm. One broadside and they're fucked. Then half a ton of ice lands on the aerial, and they have no VHF. Which is important 'cause they've cleared the prop, they get their power back, and they can dodge their way out of the storm.

Einhildur   Oh no. Because the aerial is damaged they can't tell the other two ships to turn around.

Jack   She's got it! The *Lorella* and *Roderigo* . . . all the lads are on deck chopping the ice. (*Beat.*) Fost to roll over is the *Lorella*.

Einhildur   Oh Jesus.

Jack   There was an SOS on the Morse. Then two hours later the *Roderigo*'s heard on the VHF . . . 'the whaleback's solid ice, listing badly' –

Baggie   – 'we'd like someone to come to us'.

Jack   We'd like someone to come to us.

Einhildur   Oh no!

Jack *takes out the knife.*

Jack   Forty men. All I want from you, Donald, is that middle finger of yours.

Claxton *stands.*

Baggie   Forget it, Jack.

Jack   Put your hand on the table. Your frigging finger, the finger you frig with.

Claxton *puts his hand on the table and spreads his fingers.*

Quayle   I like this. Let them both stand, in opposition to each other. The worker and the capitalist, the polar opposites of mankind, in extremis.

Einhildur *stands and, picking up the tray, whacks* **Jack** *across the head with it.* **Jack** *goes down and she dives in and rescues her kitchen knife.*

Einhildur   No! No! No! This is my knife, my hotel! Stop this madness! You . . . you . . . what is the English word for him?

Snacker   Dickhead.

Einhildur   Dickhead.

Jack *sits in the corner, head in his hands. The others sit.*

Claxton   Is it my turn?

Quayle   Hey! Yer man has a story. Jack!

Jack   Fuck off.

Quayle   No, no, I'm not having that.

He goes over to **Jack**.

Quayle   You come over here and show some respect.

Baggie   Leave him alone.

Quayle   No! I'm gonna make this man listen to his fellow man if it's the last thing I do.

He grabs **Jack**, *pulls him off his chair and drags him back to the communal table.*

Quayle   Sit yer fucking arse down.

Jack   He don't have a story.

Quayle   Listen!

Claxton   I did my first widows' walk two days ago.

Einhildur   What is this widows' walk?

Baggie (*to* **Einhildur**)   When a ship is lost the owner walks, visits every one of the widows.

Snacker   You can't drive, the kids would stab your tyres.

Baggie   It's kind of a tradition.

Quayle   It's barbaric.

Claxton   I must've walked thirty or forty mile.

Jack   Poor fucking you!

Baggie   And Stabba's wife out in the country, Sproatley.

Snacker   That's another four mile.

Baggie   Eight. Four there and four back.

Jack   Did you do it?

Baggie   Course he did.

Quayle   The man had no choice in the matter.

Claxton   Twig Williams followed me all the way. On his bike.

Baggie (*to* **Einhildur**)   Twig is a communist.

Claxton   I don't mind Twig. I started at eight in the morning, Hessle Road, the first widow, very calm, brief, didn't offer me tea, didn't look me in the eye. The next, a few doors along, a girl, twenty-one maybe, hysterical. A house full of women, one holding a baby, the girl held by her mother, and an aunt made me a cup of tea, made me drink it, and made me listen to the girl's howling, and the baby crying. Three more going west along the road, all with tea, and then the fourth, I had to ask to use the loo, and that shocked me, how incredibly wrong that felt, pissing out those first four teas in that widow's closet. And for some reason . . . no, I know the reason, I put my hand in the flow of the piss, because that's what you do, that's what deckhands do, and I'd never done it. Out of that house, and a crowd had waited for me, and then walking north towards the new estates, with Twig behind me all the way on his bike. The first house on Orchard Park was answered by a man, smoking. He went to get the woman. She was in a state of undress, or at least dressing. I had discovered a deception, an affair. I was furious, it was all I could do to stop myself barging in and giving her a piece of my mind. The next widow was only two doors along, four-year-old twins –

Baggie   – Terry's.

Claxton   There was a crucifix above the mantelpiece. The girl was silent, her mother spoke to me, gave me tea, and decency, asked me if I'd eaten, and gave me a ham sandwich with the crust cut off and, rather incredibly, a small glass of sherry. There was humanity there, empathy, and as I left she said that my father had walked to her in 1948 when she lost her husband on the *Lewis Carroll*. Tradition. From Orchard Park to Bransholme, and it started raining, and I didn't have a coat, it was clear when I'd started, and Twig behind me getting wet too. On Bransholme they all came out, all the rehoused Hessle Road families, all silent and imperious. And amazingly there's a *Hull Daily Mail* photographer, I didn't expect that, capturing my repentance. From Bransholme I walk all the way along Sutton Road to Bilton Grange, still raining, Twig behind watching me, never says a word, and I've got blisters now, and I'm limping. Three more widows on Bilton Grange, one of them wouldn't get out of bed, her mother insisted I speak to her, and pushed me up the stairs into her bedroom. When I'm done on Bilton Grange it's night and black, and I only have Stabba's wife out in Sproatley, that's four miles, country roads. And then rather comedically, Twig gets stopped by a police panda car for riding a bike without lights. Twig, being a communist, is argumentative with it and gets himself arrested. I limp off laughing, but I'm actually hysterical now, there's no Twig, I'm free and full of tea and I remember taking a piss in Holderness Drain and laughing as the urine arced away from the bank and fell the twenty feet into the water below.

And with no Twig, I'm not policed, and I nip into a minicab office and took a taxi to Sproatley.

Baggie   A taxi?!

Jack   You fucking cheat!

He stands.

Quayle   Sit your arse down.

Claxton   Yes, I cheated. I took a minicab out to Stabba's and I made the driver stop a good fifty yards from his house, so Stabba's wife wouldn't see the car. It's pitch black now, countryside dark, and I find my way down the garden path with the light coming from the living-room windows. She doesn't have her curtains drawn and I can see that she's sat looking into the fire, and as I step up to the porch to ring the bell a hand reaches out of the black and grabs my arm. I turn, expecting to see the cab driver or Twig, but it's Stabba.

Einhildur   Argh!

Claxton   Stabba himself is standing there by the porch, by their dustbin, and he grips my arm, insistent, and he looks me in the eye and says, 'Don't tell her, don't knock on the door, it'll kill her.' And I say, 'She knows already, everyone knows the *Graham Greene* is lost.' And Stabba says, 'Of course she does, but you need to understand that your knock is the end of all hope. So, don't knock, it'll kill her.' And we both look through the window and she's sat there, staring into the fire. And then the grip on my arm is gone and so is Stabba, and I don't knock, I turn and walk back to the taxi. I was done. I went home to the farm, there was no one there, my wife hasn't lived with me a couple of years now, we all know why, and I drank a bottle of whisky and slept. The next day I went to the dock offices. There was a crowd of women gathered, and all the office windows had been broken, and they saw me and started throwing stones at the car.

Jack   Taxi driver grassed you up?

Claxton   I guess. I took the train to London, and flew out here.

Quayle *stands.*

Quayle   Fuck the taxi. You did the walk. Take no notice of the women, they're brutal. You're a man in my eyes, and as good and tough a man as ever pulled on boots, and I'm proud to know you.

He slaps him on the back and shakes his hand.

Claxton   Thank you, Michael.

Baggie (*to* **Jack**)   He did the walk.

Jack   Sounds rough. All that fucking tea.

Snacker   That's my favourite! You know, if we need a winner. Donald's story.

Einhildur *turns the TV up. Quite loud.*

Jack   What's that? At this time of night.

Quayle   Morning.

Einhildur   Shhh!

Jack   Shhh! You like it, getting bossed around by a bird.

Einhildur *turns the TV volume down but leaves it on. She comes over to the men.*

Jack   Summat's happened.

Quayle   What is it, darling? Bad news.

Claxton   It's written on your face.

Einhildur   We've done it.

Jack   What have you done?

Einhildur   The Althing have voted. Our parliament. We've extended to two hundred.

Jack   What?

Quayle   Ha! Two hundred?!

Snacker   What are you on about? Two hundred what?

Claxton   Two hundred miles, national waters, exclusive fishing zone.

Baggie   That's that then.

Jack   Bastards! Where are we supposed to fish now then?!

Baggie   There's Norway.

Claxton   No. Norway voted to stay out of the Common Market. They'll do their own thing now and follow Iceland.

Baggie   Go to two hundred an'all then?

Claxton   Yup.

Jack   So we're fucked. We're all out of work!

Einhildur   Sorry.

She goes back to the bar. **Snacker** *follows her.* **Einhildur** *turns the TV off. The phone rings.*

Baggie   I'll get it! It's always me.

He goes to the phone.

Aye? . . . Aye . . . aye . . .

All   Aye . . . aye . . . aye . . . aye

Baggie   She's had the baby!

Jack/Snacker/Quayle   Woo! / Oh yes!

Baggie (*on the phone*)   Aye . . . aye . . . aye . . . aye..

Jack   What is it?!

Baggie   A girl.

Snacker   Yeah!

Baggie *holds the phone up so everyone can hear. We hear the sound of a baby crying. This rouses* **Claxton**. **Jack/Snacker/Quayle/Claxton** *give a round of applause.*

Baggie (*on phone*)   Aye . . . aye . . . aye . . . Mister Claxton's over here, and he's flying us home, yeah, London . . . aye . . . aye . . . how about that eh? . . . Aye . . . aye . . . aye . . . well done, love . . . tarra.

Phone down. He comes back to the table.

Claxton   Congratulations.

Quayle   Well done, big fellah.

Jack   How many's that now?

Baggie   Five.

Quayle (*raising a glass*)   To Mrs Baggie!

All   Mrs Baggie!

They drink. **Einhildur** *has brought a large tureen to the bar top.* **Snacker** *has the bowls. They have a whispered conversation. Head to head, forehead touching forehead.*

Jack   Eh, eh. Look at this. Fucking hell.

Quayle   The kid's a phenomenon. Special, you know, in the best way.

Snacker *picks up the fish tureen and comes to the table with it.*

Snacker   Donald.

Claxton   Yes, Snacker, what is it?

Snacker   I'm staying.

Claxton   In Iceland?

Snacker   Yeah. Here. I'm not cut out for fishing.

Jack   There in't gonna be no more fishing. Not for the likes of us.

Baggie   This is gonna kill us off.

Jack   Kill who off?

Baggie   West Hull.

Snacker   I'll run this place, with Einhildur.

Jack   You gonna marry her?

Snacker   Dunno. Do they have marriage over here?

Claxton   Good lad. I wish you the best of luck.

Snacker *goes back to the bar.*

Jack   He's gonna marry her?! Headcase.

Baggie   He's staying. That's clever.

At the bar **Snacker** *collects the plates and cutlery and takes them to the table. He leaves them without setting them and goes back to* **Einhildur**. **Einhildur** *and* **Snacker** *are in each other's arms.*

Jack   You weren't there then, Baggie? Again.

Quayle   He weren't where?

Jack   The birth. Have you been there, at that moment, for any of them?

Baggie   Not one.

Jack   That's the worst thing about fishing. You miss the best bits of your own life.

Einhildur *and* **Snacker** *kiss.*

Jack   He's kissing her! Are you watching this?

Claxton   Brilliant.

A moment of stillness, tableau. A ship's horn sounds, long and mournful. **Quayle** *begins the singing from a seated position. Then stands.*

Quayle
So long and farewell now,

Trips are all done.
No more early taxis,
To catch early tides.
So long, the trips are all done.

No more deckie learners,
The skipper has gone.
The fish room is empty
No more scratching on.
So long, the trips are all done.

So long and farewell now,
Trips are all done.
No more early taxis,
To catch early tides.
So long, the trips are all done.

No cod that need gutting
Eighteen hours a day.
No three days at home now,
With three weeks away.
So long, the trips are all done

So long and farewell now,
Trips are all done.
No more early taxis,
To catch early tides.
So long, the trips are all done.

End.

Made in United States
Orlando, FL
22 March 2026